AMERICAN TRADE LAWS AFTER THE URUGUAY ROUND

AMERICAN TRADE LAWS AFTER THE URUGUAY ROUND

GREG MASTEL

Economic Strategy Institute

M.E. Sharpe
Armonk, New York
London, England

Copyright © 1996 by M. E. Sharpe, Inc.

All rights reserved. No part of this book may be reproduced in any form without written permission from the publisher, M. E. Sharpe, Inc., 80 Business Park Drive, Armonk, New York 10504.

Library of Congress Cataloging-in-Publication Data

Mastel, Greg, 1963–
American trade laws after the Uruguay Round / Greg Mastel.
p. cm.
Includes bibliographical references and index.
ISBN 1-56324-895-6 (hardcover : alk. paper).—ISBN 1-56324-896-4 (pbk. : alk. paper)
1. Foreign trade regulation—United States.
2. Competition, Unfair—United States.
3. Dumping (International trade)—Law and legislation—United States.
4. Antidumping duties—Law and legislation—United States.
5. United States—Commercial policy.
I. Title.
KF1976.M354   1996
343.73′087—dc20
[347.30387]
96-11403
CIP

Printed in the United States of America

The paper used in this publication meets the minimum requirements of the American National Standard for Information Sciences— Permanence of Paper for Printed Library Materials, ANSI Z 39.48-1984.

| BM (c) | 10 | 9 | 8 | 7 | 6 | 5 | 4 | 3 | 2 | 1 |
| BM (p) | 10 | 9 | 8 | 7 | 6 | 5 | 4 | 3 | 2 | 1 |

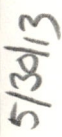

Table of Contents

List of Tables and Figures	ix
Acknowledgment	xi
1. A Pragmatic Approach to Free Trade	3

PART I
Section 301 Laws

2. U.S. Section 301 Laws	11
3. Legislative History	16
4. The Record of Section 301	20
Case Studies	21
5. The Record of Super 301	33
Case Studies	35
The Most Productive Month in Trade Negotiation History	40
6. The Record of Special 301	44
7. The Case for Extending Super 301 and Special 301	49
Initiating Cases	49
Deterrent Effect	51
8. Refutation of Major Criticisms	52
Protectionism	52
Aggressive Unilateralism	53
Trade War	54

vi   Table of Contents

9. Section 301 in the WTO Era	57
Section 301 and the WTO	57
Enforcing Trade Agreements	60
Countries Outside the WTO	61
Practices Outside the WTO	62

PART II
Antidumping Laws

10. U.S. Antidumping Laws	71
11. Rationale for Antidumping Laws	76
Overcapacity Dumping	77
Government-Supported Dumping	79
Tactical Dumping and Discriminatory Pricing	82
Predatory Dumping	84
Harassment and Biased Administration	86
12. Conclusions	93
13. The Future of Antidumping Laws	103

PART III
Countervailing Duty Laws

14. U.S. Countervailing Duty Laws	109
15. Subsidies	113
16. Subsidies around the World	118
17. Subsidies As Trade Barriers	121

18. Case Studies	127
Civilian Aerospace: Airbus	127
Steel	134
Forest Products	136
19. Countering Subsidies under U.S. Law	140
20. Countering Subsidies under International Law	145
21. Conclusions	151

Appendices

A. Section 301 Cases	155
B. Antidumping Laws around the World	174
C. Overview of Legislative Issues	175
Short-Supply Exception	175
Economies in Transition	177
Duty As Cost	178
D. International Agreements on Dumping	180
The North American Free Trade Agreement	180
The Uruguay Round Agreement	181
E. Legislative History of Antidumping Laws	186
Bibliography	189
Index	195
About the Author	207

List of Tables and Figures

Tables

2.1 Key Statutes: Section 301, Super 301, and Special 301	13
6.1 Special 301 Announcements, 1989–95	44
9.1 Section 301 and World Trade Organization Dispute Settlement	59
10.1 Summary of U.S. Dumping Determination Procedures	74
11.1 Comparison of Top Respondent Countries of Dumping Complaints (cases filed), 1984–93 and 1994–95	81
12.1 Top Respondent Countries to U.S. Section 301 Cases and Successful Final Determination of Dumping, 1985–94	94
14.1 Summary of U.S. Countervailing Duty Determination Procedures	111
16.1 Official Export Credit as a Percentage of National Exports in G-7 Countries	120
16.2 Nonagricultural Export Assistance Services of G-7 Countries, 1992	120
19.1 Affirmative Determinations in Countervailing Duty Cases, 1985–94, by Country	141

Figures

12.1 Geographic Source of Profits for Japanese Automakers   96

16.1 G-7 Countries' Total Subsidies as a Percentage of Gross Domestic Product, Including Agriculture   119

Acknowledgment

The author wishes to gratefully acknowledge the invaluable contributions of Ms. Rachel Hines in researching, writing, and editing this book and those of Ms. Lois Hayes in the final preparation for publication.

AMERICAN TRADE LAWS AFTER THE URUGUAY ROUND

Chapter One

A Pragmatic Approach to Free Trade

Anyone watching the heated public debate over such issues as the North American Free Trade Agreement (NAFTA) and trade relations with Japan might wonder, Why the fuss? Surely, free trade is one of the most universally endorsed concepts in the public policy arena. Even in an era when economic nationalism and related political movements are thought to be on the rise, the vast majority of politicians—with a few notable exceptions—endorse the principle of free trade. Modern U.S. newspaper editorial writers are almost universal in their support for it. Every economics 101 course turns out a new wave of free trade advocates each semester. Public opinion polls indicate that, despite the often cited protectionist tendencies of the American public, most Americans also endorse the concept of free trade. With free trade as universally popular as motherhood and apple pie, what's to debate?

The answer is that free trade means very different things to different people. There are two main schools of thought. First, there are unconditional free traders. Supporters of this school of thought—chiefly U.S. and British academic economists—hold that free trade is almost always positive. Consequently, they support elimination of U.S. trade barriers, even in the face of foreign protectionism. From their perspective, if other countries choose to decrease the welfare of their consumers and make themselves poorer, there is no reason for the United States to follow suit. Following a tortured extension of David Ricardo's economic thinking two centuries ago, they oppose taking any action to counter foreign governmental subsidies or predatory pricing of imports, arguing that, if foreign producers want to give U.S. consumers an inexplicably good deal on a product, the United States should take it and count its blessings. Underpinning this notion is an economic model that assumes, among other things, full employment and no barriers to industry entry—i.e., a new firm can simply enter the automobile or computer market at will.[1]

The other notion of free trade—the one to which most businessmen, most government officials, and most Americans subscribe—is a bit different. It can best be described as a reciprocal free trade. Those who subscribe to this concept believe the market is the most efficient system for allocating resources and acknowledge that international specialization can benefit all countries. They support the lowering of U.S. trade barriers, provided U.S. trading partners are willing to do likewise, but they have little interest in opening the U.S. market to countries that practice protectionism. They certainly seek the lowest price in the competitive marketplace, but—growing out of a commitment to antitrust laws and competitive markets—they are concerned about foreign efforts to gain control of markets using subsidies or predatory pricing. Consequently, they are willing to make exceptions to the general principles of free trade to counter these objectionable practices.

Supporters of the unconditional-free-trade school would have one believe that their views are derived directly from basic economic principles first outlined by Adam Smith and David Ricardo, principles as incontrovertible as the law of gravity. Their history is shaky, however. Adam Smith, for example, would clearly have put himself in the reciprocal-free-trade camp. Consider this passage from *The Wealth of Nations*:

> There may be good policy in [trade] retaliations of this kind, when there is a probability that they will procure the repeal of the high duties or prohibitions complained of. The recovery of a great foreign market will generally more than compensate the transitory inconvenience of paying dearer during a short time for some sorts of goods.[2]

Adam Smith also had strong criticism for subsidies—the targets of U.S. countervailing duty law. In fact, the notion that free trade should be unconditional has much more recent roots and is based on questionable assumptions.

The unconditional-free-trade camp has never really had much influence on public policy in the United States or in most other countries. The entire global trading system—as enshrined in the General Agreement on Tariffs and Trade (GATT)—and the dozens of major free trade agreements that have sprung up around the world are based on the concept of reciprocal free trade, not unconditional free trade. In these agreements, countries agree to lower tariffs provided that other countries do likewise. The few examples of countries pursuing unilateral free trade strategies generally are short lived, involve only a part of the overall trade picture (e.g., countries unilaterally lower tariffs in one area while raising them elsewhere or adopting new trade barriers), or, most frequently, involve countries that begin from a position of having much higher trade barriers than their trading partners. The GATT, clearly borrowing from the reciprocal-free-trade camp, includes provisions explicitly allowing countries to raise retaliatory tariffs if trading partners subsidize, engage in predatory pricing, or raise new trade barriers.

The United States' own trade laws are cut from the same cloth. The United States for decades has had legislation providing for offsetting duties on imports that are subsidized or predatorily priced—legislation known as countervailing duty law and antidumping law, respectively. Although it had been common practice for years, the United States adopted, in 1974, a formal grievance procedure that U.S. companies and others could trigger if they felt disadvantaged by foreign trade barriers. This procedure has become known as Section 301. These three trade laws—countervailing duty law, antidumping law, and Section 301—are the central pillars of American trade law.

Despite their long history, the three pillars of American trade law face continuing challenge. Many of the unconditional-free-trade school of thought have launched sharp attacks on them in recent years. Countervailing duty and antidumping laws are assailed as "process protectionism" and "monsters."[3] Section 301, which aims to open foreign markets, is denounced with more colorful terms and dubbed "aggressive unilateralism."[4] The reason for initial resistance to countervailing duty and antidumping law, from a free trade perspective, is understandable, since both result in the imposition of duties on imports. But critical analysts give scant attention to the equally large violations of free trade principles involved in government subsidies and dumping, or the foreign trade barriers that are the target of Section 301. The tone of some critics often seems uncharacteristically sharp for academic discussions. For example, one critic referred to antidumping laws as nothing more than "ordinary trade with a grand public relations strategy."[5]

When he wrote *The Wealth of Nations* 250 years ago, Adam Smith obviously was not speaking about modern American trade laws. Nonetheless, the logic he used then, which is quoted above, provides the intellectual underpinnings for the three pillars of American trade law. He would likely have viewed American trade laws not as "ordinary trade protection with a grand public relations strategy," but rather as logical tools to promote free trade. Unfortunately, Adam Smith has not played an active role in the recent debate on U.S. trade laws, and his absence has been felt. The voices of critics often seem to drown out those of defenders.

Against the background of strong criticism and attack at home and abroad, U.S. trade laws have become a major focus of international trade negotiations. In the 1988 negotiations on the U.S.-Canada Free Trade Agreement (FTA), the Canadian government made clear that its major objective was curbing the operation of U.S. antidumping and countervailing duty laws. As is explained in appendix D, Canada's efforts met with some success. Mexico demanded similar treatment when the free trade area was extended to it in 1994.

In the Uruguay Round of multilateral negotiations, Section 301 was strongly attacked by the European Community, Japan, and other trading partners—not coincidentally the targets of many Section 301 actions. Limits on antidumping laws and countervailing duty laws were also sought by some trading partners—again not coincidentally the targets of many actions under those laws. The primary objectives of the U.S. government in this latest round of multilateral trade negotiations were to gain stronger trading rules on agricultural goods and services and to win better protection of intellectual property. The United States made progress toward both of those objectives but initially made concessions that threatened American trade laws in order to achieve that progress. When the Clinton administration took over the negotiations in 1993, it fought to win back some lost ground on U.S.

trade laws, but it was still forced to accept provisions that affected the operation of each of the major trade laws.[6]

In implementing the Uruguay Round, the U.S. Congress took care to minimize the adverse impact the new trade agreement had on U.S. trade laws. In some areas it was successful, but U.S. trade laws have been weakened in other areas. Fortunately, the Uruguay Round also contained provisions that could effectively strengthen U.S. trade laws. For example, new multilateral disciplines on subsidies were introduced, and multilateral dispute settlement could, if used correctly, actually strengthen Section 301.

The net effect of the agreement will probably vary from law to law and will not fully be known until the new Uruguay Round system has had some years to operate, but clearly the Uruguay Round sparked the most significant revisions in the three pillars of American trade law in their history. With aggressive and well-considered application and defense before the WTO, however, the essential features of the three pillars can be preserved.

This book aims to analyze in detail the function of the three pillars of U.S. trade law, explain the role they play in U.S. trade policy, review the relevant provisions of the Uruguay Round, and recommend a future strategy for using Section 301, antidumping law, and countervailing duty law.[7] In short, this is an attempt to articulate once again the guiding principles behind the reciprocal-free-trade school of thought and explain how the three pillars of American trade policy can continue to provide the basis for a strong and vigorous American trade policy well into the next century.

Notes

1. Analysis of Ricardo drawn from Todd G. Bucholz, *New Ideas from Dead Economists: An Introduction to Modern Economic Thought* (New York, NY: Penguin Books, 1990), 62–85.

2. Adam Smith, *The Wealth of Nations*, book 4, chapter 2.

3. J. Michael Finger, *The Origins and Evolution of Antidumping Regulation* (Washington, DC: The World Bank, Policy, Research, and External Affairs Working Paper, 1991), 27.

4. Jagdish Bhagwati and Hugh T. Patrick, *Aggressive Unilateralism* (Ann Arbor, MI: University of Michigan Press, 1990).

5. Finger, *The Origins and Evolution of Antidumping Regulation*, cover.

6. Labor Industry Coalition for International Trade, *Implementing the Uruguay Round: What Was Achieved and How to Enact It into Law*, March 1994, 1–2.

7. It is important to note at the outset that this text does not attempt to analyze all U.S. trade laws. A number of trade laws—such as Section 201, which provides temporary import relief; Section 337, which blocks imports that infringe upon U.S. patents, trademarks, and copyrights; Section 232, which can block imports that may undermine an industry deemed critical to U.S. national security; and Section 406, which can be used to regulate imports from a nonmarket economy—are mentioned in passing but not carefully analyzed. These laws are not included for two primary reasons. First, either because the threshold for action under these statutes is very high or because administrations shy away from using these laws, they are seldom used. Second, these laws are not substantially affected by the Uruguay Round. (Section 337 is an exception to both reasons, but it was rewritten to respond to GATT decisions made before the Uruguay Round was completed and is thus beyond the scope of this book.)

Part I

Section 301 Laws

Chapter 2

U.S. Section 301 Laws*

When Carla Hills was named U.S. trade representative in 1989, President Bush jokingly handed her a crowbar as a symbol of what he wanted her to do to closed markets. Markets are not opened with crowbars, however. The actual tool used by the United States is a piece of trade legislation commonly referred to as Section 301, the trade crowbar. Over the years, the term "crowbar" has often been used to describe Section 301. It has also been described with less positive terms, ranging from "aggressive unilateralism" with the United States acting as "judge, jury, and executioner"[1] to the less charitable description of the 301 process as that of "a corrupt, bribe-taking bully."[2] All of this colorful hyperbole would lead the uninformed to think of Section 301 as a juggernaut inevitably pushing the world toward a cataclysmic trade war.

In fact, Section 301 is neither a carpenter's tool nor the trade equivalent of gunboat diplomacy. The statute and its close relatives, "Super 301" and "Special 301," are little more than a formal articulation of the powers the president has always possessed under the Constitution—the power to negotiate with foreign governments. Section 301 is simply a process whereby the administration, on its own volition or in response to a petition from U.S. parties, seeks to eliminate a foreign trade barrier. Since the passage of the Uruguay Round, the time limits and procedures for Section 301's operation have

---
*Rachel Hines contributed to this part

been modified to correspond with those of the dispute settlement procedure of the new World Trade Organization—the ultimate achievement of trade multilateralism—so that the WTO and Section 301 can work together. The harshest critic of Section 301—the European Union—is considering adoption of a similar procedure to ensure that its trade policy can work effectively with the WTO.[3]

In order to put to rest many of the misconceptions surrounding Section 301, and to explain the useful role it has played and can continue to play in American trade policy, this section of the book will analyze the statute in detail, trace its legislative history, track its record in achieving its objectives, and review the record of its close relatives, Super 301 and Special 301.

Over the last two decades, three different versions of Section 301 have been created by law. The first and most basic is Section 301 itself, which traces its history back to the Trade Act of 1974. Though it initially did little more than articulate powers the president already had to negotiate with foreign governments on trade matters, over time, it was amended to include more time limits and procedures for initiating cases (by a private-sector petition or through self-initiation by the administration). Section 301 has evolved into a process for identifying unfair foreign trade practices and initiating negotiations to eliminate those practices under the threat of trade retaliation. Its investigations are limited to twelve to eighteen months, depending on the type of trade barrier involved. (See Table 2.1 for statute cites and descriptions.)

Super 301, though only a minor variation of Section 301, is a widely discussed and highly controversial relative. It does not shorten Section 301 deadlines, nor does it make retaliation more likely. In reality, the only difference is that Super 301 requires an annual listing of both the major trade barriers confronting U.S. exporters and the countries that maintain those trade barriers. Section 301 cases must then be initiated against the trade barriers identified. Ambassador Carla Hills, U.S. trade representative (USTR) under the Bush administration, noted that Super 301 is an entirely internal process and is most similar to posting the names of trading partners that practice unfair trade "on a bulletin board."[4] Many foreign countries take umbrage at the process, however, and are greatly concerned about the prospect of being listed.

Table 2.1 **Key Statutes: Section 301, Super 301, and Special 301**

Key Statutes	Section 301	Super 301	Special 301
Enacted in	-Trade Act of 1974, Pub. L. 93-618, § 88 Stat. 2041 (1975). (19 U.S.C. 2411-2416)	-Omnibus Trade and Competitiveness Act of 1988, Pub. L. 100-418, § 102 Stat. 1164 (1988). (Amended 1974 Trade Act, section 310.)	-Omnibus Trade and Competitiveness Act of 1988, Pub. L. 100-418, § 102 Stat. 1164 (1988). (Amended 1974 Trade Act, section 182.)
Description of	Requires the USTR to investigate and respond to unfair trading practices of foreign countries, as identified by U.S. parties or the administration.	Requires the USTR to identify the countries and practices with significant trade barriers each year and initiate investigations. (Under the Clinton administration, the country identification was dropped.)	Requires the USTR to identify and initiate investigations of countries that violate intellectual property rights.
Time limits for action	12–18 months, depending on the nature of the practice.	USTR announcement April 30 of each year. (Changed to September 30 in March 1994.)	USTR announcement April 30 of each year.
Current status	Permanent legislation not requiring reauthorization.	Extended through 1997 by Executive Order.	Permanent statute. Amended to correspond with WTO time limits. Watch lists, special mention listings added.

Source: *United States Statutes at Large*, 1974, vol. 88, part 2, and vol. 102, part 2; The Uruguay Round Agreements Act of 1994, Pub. L. 103-465, 108 Stat. 4938-4943; Office of the President, "Identification of Trade Expansion Priorities Executive Order," (press release), March 3, 1994; and, Office of the United States Trade Representative, "President Extends Super 301 by Executive Order," (press release), September 28, 1995.

Super 301 was originated in the Omnibus Trade and Competitiveness Act of 1988 and was extended for 1989 and 1990.

President Clinton revived the procedure by Executive Order in 1994. Currently, Super 301 has been extended by Executive Order through 1997. The Clinton Super 301 differed from the original Super 301 in two important ways. First, the Executive Order included no provision for listing countries, only practices. Second, the Executive Order included the practice of listing countries and practices that merit possible future identification.[5]

Special 301 is essentially a mirror image of Super 301 with four differences. First, while Super 301 is directed toward any type of trade barrier, Special 301's focus is the piracy of intellectual property—patented, copyrighted, and trademarked materials—and market access barriers against the same. Second, Special 301 is a permanent annual procedure, while Super 301 has been extended only through 1997. Third, the time limits for Special 301 cases were originally shorter (six to nine months) than the normal Section 301 cases (twelve to eighteen months), but in the Uruguay Round implementing legislation, Special 301 deadlines were changed to be the same as normal Section 301 actions.[6] Finally, although there is no reference to the practice in the authorizing statute, the executive branch has created watch lists that are released in conjunction with the annual listing of Special 301 priorities. As the name suggests, these watch lists put the foreign countries on notice that they may be made a priority country in the future, and thus the topic of a Special 301 case, unless progress is forthcoming.

Notes

1. Jagdish Bhagwati and Hugh T. Patrick, *Aggressive Unilateralism* (Ann Arbor, MI: University of Michigan Press, 1990).
2. Thomas O. Bayard and Kimberly Ann Elliot, *Reciprocity and Retaliation in U.S. Trade Policy* (Washington, DC: Institute for International Economics, 1994), 320.
3. Bruce Barnard, "Brittan Says His Proposal Won't Copy U.S. Trade Act," *Journal of Commerce*, December 1, 1994, 3A.
4. Stuart Auerbach, "Hills Defends Aggressive Trade Policy; Better System Is Goal, U.S. Official Says," *Washington Post*, June 9, 1989, F2.
6. Office of the President, "Identification of Trade Expansion Priorities Executive Order," press release, March 3, 1994.
6. While intellectual property is now covered by the WTO, there may be some cases, discussed later, of intellectual property issues not covered that could still be

subject to the shorter deadlines of Special 301. The Uruguay Round Agreements Act of 1994, Pub. L. 103-465, 108 Stat. 4938-4943.

Chapter Three

Legislative History

In some sense, Section 301—or the process it enshrines in legislation—has existed since the Constitution was ratified. Over the years, there have been numerous examples of American presidents negotiating agreements with foreign countries to resolve trade matters.[1]

Since the late 1960s, however, there has been a growing sense in Congress that American exporters have not been given sufficient attention in the formation of American foreign policy, that executive branch departments—particularly the State Department and the national security bureaucracy—paid little attention to trade and economic matters. As the U.S. bilateral deficit with Japan began to grow, and the U.S. global trade surplus disappeared and was replaced with ever larger trade deficits, Congress became increasingly activist in trade policy. The Constitution specifically reserves control of trade policy for the Congress, and in 1974, Congress began to exert this authority.

This increasing congressional activism can be traced through two closely related legislative efforts. First, Congress moved to elevate the status of the U.S. trade negotiators. A number of steps were taken, including expansion of a special office with statutory responsibility to oversee trade policy and designation of cabinet status for the president's chief trade negotiator, the U.S. trade representative.[2] The primary objective of these moves was to create a powerful, institutionalized advocate for trade to counter agencies having other primary concerns, such as the State Department and the National Security Council (NSC).[3] The situation led one Reagan administration State Department official to refer to the office of USTR as "an arm of Congress."[4]

The other, more important congressional assertion of power was the creation and augmentation of Section 301. Though Section 301 was formally born in the Trade Act of 1974, similar presidential authority was extended for particular purposes in 1962.[5] Initially, Section 301 created a model for attacking foreign unfair trade practices under threat of retaliation, but the president was given broad authority to set his own deadlines and wide latitude to avoid retaliation even if negotiations failed. In addition, the clear intent of the Congress was to give considerable deference to international trade agreements.

The history of Section 301 since 1974 is essentially one of the Congress tightening its control of the process and removing presidential discretion. In the 1979 Trade Act, Congress set clear deadlines for action under Section 301 and focused on foreign trade practices that violated trade agreements. In 1984, Congress took the further step of explicitly broadening Section 301 to cover unfair trade practices involving services and intellectual property as well as trade in goods. The 1984 Trade Act also created the National Trade Estimate (NTE), an annual compilation of foreign unfair trade practices.[6]

By the mid-1980s, growing dissatisfaction with what were seen as closed markets in Japan and other major trading partners, and an increasing trade imbalance, stimulated more congressional interest in market-opening and deficit-reducing trade measures. Congressman Richard Gephardt (later to become Democratic minority leader) proposed a solution known as the Gephardt amendment that gained considerable support in the Congress, particularly in the House of Representatives. The Gephardt amendment focused on countries with which the United States had large trade deficits, requiring that the imbalances be reduced by a fixed percentage and eliminated over a period of years under threat of trade retaliation. Though this approach was widely condemned by academics, editorial writers, and others, the Gephardt amendment passed the House and was included in its version of the trade legislation that ultimately became the 1988 Trade Act.[7]

In the Senate, the Gephardt approach was widely seen as protectionist and unworkable. Another proposal, known as Super 301, was originally sponsored by Senators Danforth, Riegle, Byrd, and Dole and had the vast majority of support.[8] This amendment was very similar to the Super 301 that ultimately became law—a procedure to identify foreign trade barriers and the countries that maintain them, and to initiate Section 301 cases against them.[9] The only major difference between the initial amendment and the resulting Super 301 legislation was a provision that allowed the Senate Finance Committee and the House Ways and Means Committee to initiate Section 301 investigations by passing a resolution. This provision was dropped in conference with the House.

In addition to creating Super 301, the 1988 Trade Act made a number of important changes to Section 301. The statute created Special 301. It also gave the USTR the central statutory role in making decisions on certain issues, including if and how to retaliate. As a practical matter, this step was more symbolic than real. As a member of the administration, a USTR would not act without consulting the rest of the administration, but putting the USTR at the center of the process, it was hoped, would further enhance the stature of the position. The 1988 Trade Act also made retaliation mandatory in Section 301 cases involving violations of trade agreements.[10] This provision further reinforced a distinction between "unjustifiable" trade barriers that were violations of trade agreements, and "unreasonable" trade barriers, which were those judged as unfair by the United States.

The only major revisions to Section 301 since the 1988 Trade Act came in the implementing legislation for the Uruguay Round in 1994. In general, this legislation completed the linkage between Section 301 and the WTO dispute settlement process, but it included three other provisions of note. First, it urged the administration to continue using Section 301 aggressively on issues not covered, or inadequately covered, by the Uruguay Round Agreement. Second, in order to bring it into compliance with the dispute settlement time limits set in the WTO, the shorter Special 301 time limits of six to nine months were lengthened to match the normal Section 301 time limits.[11] Finally, the implementing bill included a one-year extension of Super 301. Clinton had already extended Super 301 by Executive Order earlier in 1994, so the statute merely reflected what the president had already voluntarily put in place.[12] The extension matched the so-called Clinton version of Super 301, which dropped the provision requiring the naming of countries and focused only on barriers, in the hope that it would be viewed as a less provocative act without losing its efficacy.[13] Clinton extended Super 301 for a second time in September 1995, for two years.

Notes

1. Section 301 legislative history from: *U.S. Statutes at Large, 1974*, vol. 88, part 2, and 1988, vol. 102, part 2; *Overview and Compilation of U.S. Trade Statutes*, Committee on Ways and Means, U.S. House of Representatives, 1993, 72–82; The Uruguay Round Agreements Act of 1994, Pub. L. 103-465, 108 Stat. 4938-4943.

2. Steven Dryden, *Trade Warriors* (New York, NY: Oxford University Press, 1995).

3. Two good examples of the conflicting interest between administrative agencies were provided during the debate over whether to list Japan under Super 301 in 1989 (see Stuart Auerbach, "Global Stakes High as Decision on Japan Trade Nears," *Washington Post*, May 25, 1989, C12; and Stuart Auerbach, "Bush Hears Debate on Japan Trade; Advisors Dispute 'Unfair' Label," *Washington Post*, May 23, 1989, C1) and during the debate in 1994 to reinstate Super 301 (see Peter Behr, "Clinton Aims a Warning Shot on Trade—Away from Japan," *Washington Post*, March 4, 1994, B1).

4. Conversations of the author.

5. Trade Expansion Act of 1962, §252, Pub. L. 87-794, 75 Stat. 879.

6. Trade and Tariff Act of 1984, Pub. L. 98-573, 98 Stat. 2948.

7. Claude E. Barfield, "Brother of Gephardt," *Washington Post*, March 9, 1988, A25; Hobart Rowen, "'Gephardt II's' Meat Ax Approach to Trade," *Washington Post*, September 15, 1991, H01.

8. The amendment passed the Senate by a vote of 89–11.

9. Barfield, "Brother of Gephardt," A25.

10. With some exceptions for national security, etc.

11. Previous to the WTO, intellectual property provisions were not included in the GATT, so time limits to match the GATT were then unnecessary.

12. In late 1995, several efforts were made in Congress to extend the authorizing legislation for Super 301, but none has yet become law.

13. The Uruguay Round Agreements Act of 1994, Pub. L. 103-465, 108 Stat. 4938-4943.

Chapter Four

The Record of Section 301

By April 1996, Section 301 had been used 101 times. Appendix A lists the cases and gives a brief summary of the actions and their outcome. Given that Section 301 has been used in such a wide variety of ways and with such widely differing levels of commitment by administrations over the years, a mere recitation of the cases is not particularly meaningful. Although the majority of the cases have been settled to the satisfaction of the U.S. industry involved and the U.S. trade negotiators, the success or failure of a case is a subjective judgment. Results are often difficult to quantify since actual trade flows depend on a number of factors, and Section 301 sometimes strips away one set of barriers only to reveal others. There can be little doubt, however, that Section 301 has been an important tool in opening markets and expanding U.S. exports. Section 301's ultimate source of leverage is the threat to close the U.S. market. Just the threat of Section 301 action, including recourse to multilateral dispute settlement, is sometimes sufficient to convince trading partners to open their market.

To shed more light on the record of the statute, four representative Section 301 cases have been chosen to illustrate how Section 301 can work and when it is likely to fail. The case studies were also chosen to illustrate the connection between Section 301 and the GATT dispute settlement procedure in order to demonstrate the possible working relationship between Section 301 and the WTO. The results of Super 301 and Special 301 are separately reviewed.

Case Studies

China Market Access, 1991

One of the most significant uses of Section 301 was the 1991 case to address a variety of market access barriers in China.[1] This case is of interest for three reasons. First, in terms of both the scope and the volume of trade involved, this was perhaps the largest Section 301 case ever pursued. When Super 301 was passed, its Senate authors made it clear that they envisioned broadly focused cases such as this one, but most of the cases actually undertaken under Super 301 had been narrowly focused on a particular product or a particular practice. Though the China case was not pursued under Super 301, it is perhaps the best example of how Super 301 was supposed to work. This has led some to conclude that Super 301 is unnecessary. This conclusion, however, neglects the other factors that led to the success of this case.

Second, since China was not a member of the GATT, this case was unique in that there was never an issue of working in conjunction with a GATT dispute settlement panel or somehow undermining the GATT by acting bilaterally. Interestingly, at this point, China was also interested in joining the GATT (now the WTO)—a process over which the United States had, and still has, considerable influence. U.S. trade negotiators were able to use the prospect of entry into the GATT as leverage to obtain the removal of trade barriers investigated in the Section 301 case.

Finally, the domestic political context of this case was unique. The Bush administration undertook the Section 301 action at a time when Congress was considering legislation to strip Chinese goods of Most Favored Nation tariff status, which would have the effect of raising U.S. tariffs on Chinese goods to prohibitive levels. In return for their support of continuing MFN status for China, a number of U.S. senators insisted that the Bush administration act under Section 301 to address Chinese trade barriers. Given the reluctance of the Bush administration to use Section 301, it is unlikely that action would have been taken were it not for the leverage of Congress in this instance.

After long and fruitless consultations, Ambassador Carla Hills initiated the Section 301 investigation into China's market access barriers on October 10, 1991. As noted, the scope of the case was quite broad, including China's:
1) failure to publish relevant laws, regulations, judicial decisions, and administrative decisions;
2) product and sector-specific import bans and quantitative restrictions;
3) import licensing requirements;
4) technical barriers to trade, including discriminatory technical and testing barriers, and sanitary and phytosanitary barriers; and
5) policy of import substitution.

The goal of the case, as articulated by congressional leaders, was to put an end to the extensive trade barriers that block imports.[2]

The negotiations dragged on fruitlessly for some time. In August of 1992, the Bush administration threatened to retaliate against almost $4 billion in Chinese imports to the United States. This was not required by the 301 statute, but the Bush administration wanted to convince China that it was serious about taking action if an agreement was not reached. An unstated reason for the administration's action was the desire to convince Congress—which was still considering MFN action—that President Bush was willing to "get tough" with China. Whatever the motive, the tactic worked. After dutifully threatening to counter-retaliate against U.S. exports, China reached an agreement with U.S. negotiators on the day retaliation was threatened—October 10, 1992. China agreed to end its policy of import substitution, make public all relevant laws and regulations, and end discriminatory testing and sanitary barriers. It also agreed to end import licenses, import bans, and other import controls on hundreds of products. The phase out of barriers was to begin on December 31, 1992, and to be completed by December 31, 1997.

The agreement was definitely a step toward opening the Chinese market. The office of the USTR notes that China has eliminated 800 nontariff barriers—258 of which were covered by the agreement—since December 31, 1993. The USTR also credits China with streamlining the import approval process and eliminating import controls. On the strength of these steps, and while noting several compliance problems, the USTR judged that China was "in substantial compliance with the agreement."[3] The ultimate impact of the agreement on trade flows is impossible to determine at this point or perhaps ever, but deputy USTR Michael Moskow suggested the agreement might ultimately result in several billion dollars' worth of new U.S. exports to China annually.[4] Though trade problems still exist in China and continuing enforcement will be critical, the consensus of U.S. businesses operating in China and other informed observers is that the agreement has made progress.

This case is unique in many respects, but it clearly demonstrates the effectiveness of Section 301 as a tool to open markets—particularly in those cases where mediation by an international trade body is impossible and U.S. resolve is firm. As noted at the outset, one author recently declared that the success of normal Section 301 in this instance proves the statutory demands of Super 301 are not necessary to ensure that major cases are launched.[5] This assertion is discussed in more detail later, but it is based on a very selective reading of the facts surrounding this case. If it were always possible to assume that the unique factors involved in this case—congressional pressure and leverage stemming from the MFN decision, the Bush administration's desire to demonstrate resolve vis-à-vis China, and China's desire to join the GATT—would be present, this argument would have some validity. Not only does this coincidence not occur regularly, but nothing similar has ever occurred. If the United States can only pursue an effective Section 301 policy when these extraordinary events coincide, it is safe to say the United States will never pursue an effective Section 301 policy without Super 301.

Canadian Beer, 1990

The 1990 Section 301 case against the Canadian (Ontario and Quebec) provincial liquor boards' discrimination against U.S. beer imports demonstrates the necessity of strong U.S. trade laws even in those instances where multilateral trade dispute settlement is available. In this trade dispute, while the United States had two GATT panels rule in its favor—and partially positive rulings under the Canada-U.S. Free Trade Agreement on dumping—the United States was still forced to impose trade sanctions under Section 301, a move sanctioned by the

GATT panel, to convince Canada to end its discriminatory practices against American beer.[6]

In May of 1990, the G. Heileman Brewing Company filed a Section 301 petition stating that the Canadian provincial liquor boards restricted beer imports through listing requirements, fees, and distribution restrictions. The USTR initiated an investigation in June of 1990 and simultaneously requested consultations under the GATT. Canada had been previously the subject of an identical GATT case filed by the European Community (EC) against the liquor boards, and now the United States pressed Canada to commit to a timeline for implementation of the EC case panel decision. During this time, an additional petition was filed in the United States by another brewing company against the Canadian practices. Because of Canada's unwillingness to comply with the EC panel ruling, the United States requested that a new dispute settlement panel be established. Canada agreed to the panel in January 1991.[7] Meanwhile, in January of 1991, three Canadian brewers brought dumping cases against Heileman, Strohs, and Pabst to the Canadian International Trade Tribunal (CITT, the Canadian equivalent of the U.S. International Trade Commission), which then allowed for the imposition of antidumping duties against the U.S. brewers.[8]

The GATT panel considering the Canadian provincial trade barriers ruled in favor of the United States in October of 1991 and released a report with specific action required of Canada. It was clear that if Canada failed to comply by March 1992, the United States was authorized to suspend concessions. In March, Canada agreed to the terms but proposed a one-year phase-in period. The USTR, unsatisfied with the length of time, announced that duties would be imposed on Canadian beer at the end of April 1992. Canada sought further discussions, and eventually an Agreement in Principle was signed by both countries to reduce the barriers against U.S. imports. Unfortunately, by this time new Canadian restrictions had been placed on imported and domestic beer through an environmental levy on beer cans. While the duty applied to both domestic and imported beer, it effectively discriminated against American imports, which are more likely to be in cans than Canadian beer, which tends to be bottled.[9]

In July 1992 the United States imposed duties of 50 percent ad valorem on beer from Ontario, the province with the most restrictive and GATT-illegal practices.[10] Ignoring the GATT ruling, Canada responded to the sanctions by imposing the same increase (50 percent) on imports into Ontario brewed by Heileman and Strohs (the other petitioner of the case).[11]

In May and June of 1993 the USTR requested the talks be resumed, and in August of 1993 an agreement was reached by the Canadian trade minister and the USTR that gave U.S. brewers access to the Ontario market by removing fees and allowing access to Ontario Brewers Retail, Inc. (which oversaw the sales of beer in the province). The agreement also removed the minimum price requirements to allow U.S. brewers to compete and required review of all duties imposed on Heileman and Strohs under the dumping determination, but Canada was not required to rescind the environmental levy. Once this agreement was signed, the United States removed the duties it had imposed on Canadian beer.

In the past year and a half, Canadian actions have threatened the agreement. In November of 1993, Quebec was singled out as a violator of the minimum price requirements, and in January of 1994, Heileman and Strohs complained of continued discrimination in all provinces, especially Ontario.[12] Consultations were resumed under the Memorandum of Understanding (MOU). In May of 1994, some allowances were made to U.S. brewers, allowing U.S. beer to be sold in supermarkets for the first time, but the minimum price requirements problem was not resolved.[13] As part of the review agreed to in the MOU, the CITT found that Canadian brewers were no longer injured by American beer imports, and that dumping duties should be lifted. In January of 1995, Canadian brewers appealed this decision under the CFTA binational panels, but the panel affirmed the CITT decision on November 15, 1995.[14]

The Canadian beer case is an excellent example of all that can go wrong, even with arbitration under international trade agreements. In virtually every instance the United States had a legitimate case against the Canadian government and was backed up by two GATT panels as well as the decision previously won by the EC. Without Section 301, the United States would have had no way of enforcing panel decisions and no recourse against Canada's violation of the GATT.

Japanese Citrus, 1988

In May of 1988, the USTR launched a Section 301 case against Japan's restrictive quotas for oranges and orange juice.[15] This was in response to a petition filed by the Florida Citrus Industry after negotiations with the Japanese on citrus broke down. The citrus industry complained that quotas, and an additional requirement that orange juice imports be blended with domestically produced juice, were "unjustifiable" trade restrictions. At the same time, dispute settlement procedures were requested under the GATT. For years prior to the Section 301 investigation, Japan and the United States had been meeting on this issue. After much time and many broken promises, Section 301 was launched. Within two months, the Japanese ambassador to the United States had presented a plan for the phasing out of quotas on oranges and orange juice imports, the relaxation of the blending requirement, and the added reduction of tariffs on grapefruits and lemons. This agreement was acceptable to both the U.S. government and the citrus industry, and by September the case was closed.

Reasons for the success of this case are numerous. The agreement allowed for the gradual elimination of the import quotas for oranges by 1991 and for orange juice by 1992. This phase-in period for implementation made the agreement much more politically plausible for the Japanese government, recently under attack from the powerful farm lobby in Japan.[16] It was also clear to the Japanese government that it would lose the case at the GATT, and blocking the decision would surely invoke retaliation by the United States under Section 301. Past successes by the United States in winning favorable rulings against the (then) European Community's agricultural import restrictions made the Japanese case that much weaker and made defeat more certain. More directly, in 1986 a case was filed under the GATT against Japan's restrictive policies on twelve other agricultural products, including fruit juices, and in late 1987 the panel ruled against these policies.[17] Another unfavorable ruling at the GATT for Japan would only increase their growing problems—with the Japanese farm groups who were protesting the GATT decision and demanding that Japan ignore the ruling, and with its trading partners, already frustrated over their trade deficits with Japan.

Political pressure in the United States also signaled Japan that the United States was serious about this case. In 1988, the trend within the United States and the Congress was for stronger trade laws—specifically in response to Japan's large trade imbalance and unfair trade practices.[18] In addition, 1988 was an election year, and the Reagan administration did not want to look weak in its dealings with Japan, nor did it want to leave this dispute unresolved for the incoming administration.[19]

The brevity of the case, and the satisfaction reached by both sides, indicates willingness on the part of the Japanese to avoid a major trade dispute at the GATT and also gives evidence that Section 301 was perceived as a powerful negotiating tool. Years of negotiations did not accomplish the response that the opening of a Section 301 investigation did. In this example, the United States almost certainly would have won at the GATT, but Section 301 made a panel settlement unnecessary.

European Oilseeds, 1987

The Section 301 case filed against the European Community with regard to oilseeds subsidies is a prime example of multilateral trade dispute settlement and Section 301 working hand in hand, and it also underlines the importance of unwavering protection to American interests if negotiations are to succeed. In this case, the United States had completely exhausted GATT remedies before employing threats of retaliation. Section 301 played an important role in keeping United States, European, and GATT efforts focused on the problem, but because it was not aggressively utilized, Section 301 did not achieve a satisfactory agreement. The failure of this case was the result of a number of factors—unwise concessions made in the so-called Blair House Agreement, pressure within the United States to complete the Uruguay Round Agreement and to stave off trade conflict with Europe, and internal disputes within the European Community. The oilseeds case highlighted the problems within the GATT before the Uruguay Round and certainly stimulated progress toward stronger agricultural guidelines, as well as a more binding dispute settlement procedure, in the Uruguay Round Agreement.[20]

After petitions were filed by the American Soybean Association in 1987, the USTR opened an investigation into practices by the European Community to protect and promote domestic oilseed production. Previously, during the Dillon Round of multilateral trade negotiations in 1961, the United States and the EC had agreed to reciprocal tariff concessions on oilseeds, but at the time, demand in the EC was high and production low. In 1966, the EC attempted to stimulate the oilseeds market with price subsidization, which did not increase their production until the 1980s.

Section 301 cases against the EC's agricultural practices were not rare. In fact, of the 101 Section 301 cases launched, 21 were agriculture-related cases filed against the EC. Often the GATT ruled in favor of the United States, stating that the policies of the Common Agricultural Policy (CAP) were in violation of nondiscriminatory treatment guaranteed to the United States under the GATT.[21] Quite frequently, the EC would abide by the decision and implement the change only to increase subsidies in favor of another agricultural product or to the processors of the original agricultural product. In this case, though, the EC simply refused to address the oilseeds problem.

Consultations under the GATT began with the EC in 1988, and by May, the USTR requested a formal dispute settlement panel. The EC stalled the process to the point that a full year went by without the appointment of members to the panel. The panel was finally assembled, and in December of 1990 it ruled in favor of the United States, stating that the policies of the EC were inconsistent with the GATT. The EC agreed to the provisions of the decision but wanted to implement them as part of the Uruguay Round Agreement scheduled for completion by December of 1990. Because the agreement was not concluded when expected, the new policies were not implemented.

Over the next two years, the EC instead shifted the subsidy from the oilseed processors to the oilseed producers, thus instituting yet another barrier against United States oilseed exporters. In 1992, the USTR asked for the GATT panel to be reconvened. The panel again ruled that the behavior of the EC denied the United States the agreed upon trade concessions, and due to the inaction by the EC, retaliation was threatened by the United States. Three more months of discussions between the United States and the EC began, launched by the promise of compensation to the United States for damages. This held off any retaliatory action, but now in dispute was the amount of compensation; the United States estimated damage to the oilseed industry to be $2 billion, but the EC offered only $400 million in damages. The USTR went to the GATT and requested permission for the suspension of concessions. Again, the EC blocked the decision.[22]

After four years, countless meetings, and exhaustion of all the available remedies of the GATT, preparations were made in the United States to raise duties by 200 percent on 300 million dollars' worth of EC imports (wine, rapeseed oil, wheat gluten). The reaction by Europe was predictably negative, and a last-ditch effort was made by the United States to resolve the issue, which led to the Blair House Agreement of November 1992. The agreement reduced, in a number of ways, the amount of land that would qualify for the oilseeds subsidy, and certain producers were no longer eligible. The last two points provided for the Blair House Agreement to be included in the Uruguay Round Agreement and for the United States to forgo any claim for compensation.

Though the EC in general and the French in particular expressed dissatisfaction, the agreement was actually a poor settlement for the United States. U.S. trade negotiators were heavily invested in the completion of the Uruguay Round and were frustrated by two years of unsuccessful efforts to end the negotiations. The United States was also in the middle of a presidential election, and the prospect of leaving the task undone when power was transferred loomed large. Problems within the EC were more apparent after the agreement was reached. France was profoundly unhappy with the agreement and, with a more conservative government newly in office, demanded a reopening of the Blair House Agreement early in 1993 and threatened to block its implementation that spring if it was not renegotiated. Farm groups in the United States were more justifiably disappointed with the agreement, but they realized that reopening the agreement was unlikely to result in further progress and pressured the administration not to renegotiate. In the end, a few more concessions were made, France agreed, the EC ratified the agreement, and the USTR closed the investigation, though continuing to monitor the situation.

The Blair House decision left the United States with no compensation for lost revenue from the subsidies during the years of the dispute, and the weak agreement, which did not fully eliminate the problem, was then incorporated into the Uruguay Round Agreement. This is an example where multilateral efforts were tried and failed, but without the pressure of Section 301 to keep the focus on the issue here and abroad, even this modest agreement would have been unlikely. Had retaliation been imposed, the result may have been better ultimately. The oilseeds case demonstrates that Section 301 can effectively augment and backstop multilateral trade dispute settlement. It is true that many of the weaknesses of GATT dispute settlement were addressed by the subsequent WTO. However, nothing in the new WTO itself could move the EC much further than the GATT—the EC had already been found culpable by two international panels in the soybean case. Only the threat of retaliation under Section 301 moved them to action. Despite what the overheated rhetoric on the new WTO suggests, the organization has no police force and no ability to dictate change in national laws. In most cases, the threat of retaliation under Section 301 is the only real leverage the United States has.

Notes

1. China market access case history from: Office of the USTR, semi-annual *Report to Congress on Section 301 Developments Required by Section 309 (a) (3) of the Trade Act of 1974,* January-December 1993; public case files of the USTR #301-88; and Office of the USTR, *1994 National Trade Estimate Report on Foreign Trade Barriers* (Washington, DC: USTR, 1994), 43–57.

2. "A Biggish Stick: Chinese-American Trade," *The Economist*, October 19, 1991, 26.

3. Quote is from the Office of the USTR, *Report to Congress on Section 301 Developments Required by Section 309 (a) (3) of the Trade Act of 1974,* January-December 1993, 4. During a recent trade dispute with the United States over WTO accession, China briefly suspended the 1992 agreement, but in early March 1995 China agreed to reapply the terms of the agreement. Bilateral consultations on agreement enforcement have recently intensified.

4. "11th Hour Deal Averts Trade War," *South China Morning Post*, October 12, 1992, 1.

5. Thomas O. Bayard and Kimberly Ann Elliot, *Reciprocity and Retaliation in U.S. Trade Policy* (Washington, DC: Institute for International Economics, 1994), 318.

6. Canadian beer case history from USTR: public case file, #301-80; Office of the USTR, *Report to Congress on Section 301 Developments Required by Section 309 (a) (3) of the Trade Act of 1974,* January-December 1993; Office of the USTR, *1994 National Trade Estimate Report on Foreign Trade Barriers* (Washington, DC: USTR, 1994), 27–29.

7. Canada also brought a complaint to the GATT for discriminatory practices by individual U.S. state tax policies on liquor (beer) distribution. In this case, the GATT panel ruled, in February of 1992, that some of these practices were in violation of the GATT.

8. In September and October of 1991, Heileman filed two Requests for Panel Review under the U.S.-Canada Free Trade Agreement in response to the determination of injury and determination of dumping. Under the CFTA, binational panels may be formed and, in the case of dumping, must determine if the decision is legal based on the law of the individual country. The decision in these two cases, made in August and September of 1992, ruled against some of the determinations by CITT but ultimately in favor of the imposition of duties by Canada, whereas later, a GATT panel ruled against Canada on the dumping issue (*Federal Register*, vol. 56, no. 219; vol. 57, no. 164; vol. 57, no. 176; vol. 57, no. 224).

9. "Aluminum: Ontario Drags Aluminum into Beer War," *Metals Week*, May 25, 1992, 10; Bob Regan, "Beer Can War Not Bottled Up; Washington Spews Hints of New Action," *American Metals Market*, June 17, 1993, 1.

10. At this time, the United States also requested a GATT panel be established in response to the antidumping duties imposed by Canada in 1991. The ruling again came out in favor of the United States under the Antidumping Code in April of 1994 ("GATT Panel 'Remands' Beer Dispute," *NAFTA Watch*, April 29, 1994, 5).

11. Keith Bradsher, "Canada Beer Dispute Flares on Eve of Trade Talks," *New York Times*, July 25, 1992, 35.

12. "U.S./Canada Beer Dispute," *NAFTA Watch*, January 19, 1994, 8.

13. "U.S., Canada Reach Agreement on Market Access for U.S. Beer," *NAFTA Watch*, May 16, 1994, 6.

14. *Inside U.S. Trade*, January 13, 1995, 1; Article 1904, Binational Panel Review Pursuant to the North American Free Trade Agreement, "Decision of the Panel on Review of the Canadian International Trade Tribunal Finding," CDA-95-1904-01.

15. Japanese citrus case history from: USTR public case file #301-66.

16. Damon Darlin, "Japan's Farm Lobby Fighting Reforms by Exploiting National Distrust of U.S.," *Wall Street Journal*, July 7, 1988; Stuart Auerbach, "Japan Stalls Response to GATT Finding; Nation Tries to Block Portions of Trade Ruling," *Washington Post*, December 3, 1987, C01.

17. Stuart Auerbach, "Trade Panel Backs U.S. on Complaint Against Japan; GATT Unit Rules That Imports of Many Agricultural Products Unfairly Restricted," *Washington Post*, November 5, 1987, E02.

18. The congressional debate on the Trade Act of 1987 (not passed but reintroduced as the 1988 Trade Act) and the Trade Act of 1988 are full of references to Japan's trade surplus with the United States. Starting in 1985, see Hearing Report, "Action to Respond to the Unfair Trade Practices of Japan and to Reduce the Trade Deficit," U.S. House Ways and Means Committee, April 1, 1985; Hearing Report, "Presidential Authority to Respond to Unfair Trade Practices, Title II," U.S. Senate Finance Committee, July 22, 1986; and Hearing Report, "Improving Enforcement of Trade Agreements," U.S. Senate Finance Committee, March 17, 1987.

19. John T. Norman, "U.S. Study Ordered of Japanese Curb on Orange Imports," *Wall Street Journal*, May 26, 1988.

20. EC oilseeds case history from: USTR public case file #301-63; Office of the USTR, semi-annual *Report to Congress on Section 301 Developments Required by Section 309 (a) (3) of the Trade Act of 1974,* July-December 1991; James R. Arnold, "The Oilseeds Dispute and the Validity of Unilateralism in a Multilateral Context," *Stanford Journal of International Law,* 1994, vol. 30:187.

21. See cases #4, 8, 11, 25, 26, 63 in Appendix A.

22. Prior to the WTO, one country alone could veto a decision from being adopted by the GATT.

Chapter Five

The Record of Super 301

For all the controversy surrounding it, Super 301 has quite a short record. As mentioned, it was authorized originally only for 1989 and 1990; President Clinton revived it by Executive Order for 1994 and 1995.[1] In 1995, The Clinton administration again extended Super 301 by Executive Order for 1996 and 1997. In 1990, however, Super 301 was not implemented. The Bush administration declared there were no trade problems to justify the naming of priority foreign countries or priority foreign practices—a strange announcement given that a sweeping Section 301 case was initiated against China the next year.[2] Ambassador Carla Hills surprised many by testifying before Congress that Japan had reformed its trade practices and no longer deserved to be targeted under Super 301.[3] The Bush administration argued that using Super 301 might endanger the imminent conclusion of the Uruguay Round, which did not, in fact, conclude until December of 1993.[4]

In 1994, the Clinton administration only partially implemented Super 301. Trade tensions had been quite high with Japan throughout the year, and the Executive Order was announced just after a failed summit meeting between President Clinton and the Japanese prime minister. As the deadline for action under Super 301 approached, however, there was a hurried attempt to address bilateral trade issues such as flat glass, forest products, and auto parts.[5] Flat glass was addressed through bilateral negotiations, which resulted in an agreement, the commercial value of which has yet to be proven. Forest products were placed on a watch list for possible future action. The administration initiated a Section 301 investigation of Japanese auto parts barriers, but, to appease the Japanese, initiated it outside of the Super 301 rubric. The practical difference between self-initiating a Section 301 case independently—authority the USTR always has—and initiating it under Super 301 is nil, but there was apparently a political difference in the minds of some. Some in Congress criticized the decision to avoid employing Super 301 as excessive sensitivity to Japanese concerns and little sensitivity to the intent of the statute.[6] In 1995, no new cases were initiated. An agreement was struck with Korea, however, aimed at opening the Korean auto market days before the Super 301 decision was announced. Although China and Japan both appeared on the Super 301 warning list no further action was initiated.[7]

This short recitation of its history makes one point clear: Super 301 was fully implemented in only one year—1989—by the Bush administration. Even in that year, the administration took care to implement it in a very focused way, hitting only limited and discrete foreign trade barriers, rather than the sweeping, systemic trade problems that were the targets intended by Congress. In the case of Japan, the Bush administration chose to address systemic barriers through a new, bilateral dialogue clumsily titled the Structural Impediments Initiative, or SII.[8]

In 1989, the administration identified three priority countries: Japan, Brazil, and India. With regard to Japan, three sectors were identified: forest products, satellites, and supercomputers. In Brazil, the objective was the elimination of the system of import licenses on all imported products—the closest example of the vision Congress had for Super 301. In India, two sectors where protectionism was quite blatant were identified: insurance and investment.[9]

The political reality dictated that Japan be a necessary target of Super 301. Early versions of the legislation actually named Japan and attached unflattering titles, such as "adversarial trader."[10] The legislative history was quite clear—there was widespread concern in the business community, and the bilateral trade imbalance with Japan was swelling. Japan was assumed to be a target, but the naming of

Brazil and India was more of a surprise. Though both practiced extensive protectionism, their markets were quite small, and they had not been the focus of the trade debate. In all likelihood, the naming of Brazil and India ultimately had more to do with diplomatic concerns than trade policy, as there was a desire on the part of the Bush administration to avoid embarrassing Japan by singling it out.[11] Other nations, such as Taiwan and Korea, that were considered likely candidates were not named because agreements were struck with them to address many key trade problems.[12] Thus, almost by the process of elimination, Brazil and India were left. Most of the attention, however, and negotiating resources devoted to Super 301 were focused on Japan.

Despite its obvious lack of enthusiasm for Super 301, the Bush administration's three choices of cases to pursue with Japan under Section 301 were sound ones. The largest of the three involved a variety of barriers Japan used to discourage imports of finished wood products, including building standards that discouraged the use of wood, and testing and certification procedures that discriminated against imported wood products. Though they were not listed in the initial Section 301 filing, trade restrictive tariffs on manufactured wood product imports also became a major focus of the case.

Case Studies

Japanese Wood Products, 1989

The trade situation in wood products is unique from a number of perspectives, not the least of which is that, although Japan had erected a system of barriers to exclude processed wood products, it was a voracious importer of unprocessed wood products: logs.[13] In fact, since Japan has very little harvestable timber of its own, the Japanese forest products industry is almost entirely dependent on foreign sources of logs. Furthermore, since almost every other country with forest resources has banned or restricted log exports, the United States is the primary source of logs for Japan. The exportation of raw logs is politically controversial in the United States, and the export of logs cut from government land is already prohibited. This puts the Japanese industry in the awkward position of needing to keep the U.S. forest products industry happy in order to ensure a supply of logs, while excluding finished forest product exports from the United States to maintain a market for Japanese production.[14]

A superficial analysis of the situation would lead one to believe that the Japanese wood product manufacturing industry is more efficient than its U.S. counterparts, this being the only way to explain the ability of the Japanese industry to compete while depending on imported raw materials from across the Pacific. This is not the case, however. Japanese mills tend to be very small in comparison to U.S. lumber mills, and the technology employed is at least a decade behind that in the United States. A 1989 Commerce Department study of the competitive conditions in the industry found the U.S. forest products industry was much more efficient than its Japanese counterparts.[15]

In the Commerce Department's view, the survival of the Japanese forest products industry depended on trade barriers. Japanese trade barriers ranged from construction standard to standards and testing requirements. These standards strongly biased construction in Japan—particularly in Japan's urban areas—away from wood and toward other construction materials. Japan argued that these construction standards were necessary because of the threat of earthquakes and fire in urban areas, but testing in other areas subject to urban crowding and earthquakes found wood to be as safe, and in many cases safer, than other construction materials. Another problem cited in Japan is the escalating tariff scales, with no, or very low, tariffs on logs and unfinished products and higher tariffs on finished products. The tariff issue was not included in the original Super 301 announcement because the tariffs were within the GATT-bound rates and thus were not, for lack of a better term, unfair. However, both the forest industry and the Commerce Department officials involved in the negotiations saw the tariffs as central to the system of Japanese trade barriers and successfully pressed for them to be raised in the negotiations. Over the long term, the Commerce Department estimated that the elimination of all the Japanese trade barriers, including tariffs, could result in *at least* a $1 billion increase in U.S. wood product exports.[16]

The wood products case was the last of the three Japanese Super 301 cases to be settled. No doubt a significant factor in pushing Japan toward settlement was the prospect of being identified under Super 301 again in 1990. The agreement eventually reached with Japan, hailed by the U.S. industry, Congress, and other observers as a substantial victory, called upon Japan, among other things, to move its construction standards toward performance-based standards and away from simple prohibitions on the use of wood. Japan also agreed to lower tariffs on manufactured wood products as part of the agreement to conclude the Uruguay Round of trade negotiations.

Unfortunately, the agreement did not result in the increased level of wood product exports that was anticipated. There were several likely causes for this disappointing result. First, macroeconomic factors, primarily Japan's greatly reduced growth rate over the period, slowed Japan's construction rates. Second, as is the case in sectors as diverse as semiconductors and beef, Japanese protectionism runs many layers deep. Eliminating the first level of barriers is not always enough to yield results. The U.S. wood products industry complains that building regulations are still slanted against wood, and distribution of imported wood products is blocked by a byzantine distribution system. It has also been quite difficult to convince Japan to fulfill its promised tariff cuts. As a result of the continuing Japanese protectionism in this sector, the office of the U.S. trade representative warned the Japanese government in 1994 that further action under Super 301 is a possibility in the future. In response to U.S. complaints, Japan has pointed out that since tariff concessions began, there has been a 100 percent increase in U.S. wood product exports. In sector after sector, it is clear that battling Japanese trade barriers normally takes several rounds to succeed. Hopefully, with continuing efforts by the administration, the U.S. industry, and the Japanese, the wood products agreement will fulfill its potential.[17]

Japanese Supercomputers and Satellites, 1989

The other two Super 301 cases launched against Japan in 1989 were much smaller in economic terms than the wood products case, but they involved high-technology products—supercomputers and satellites—arguably of considerable strategic importance. In both cases, the focus was Japanese government procurement policies that appeared slanted toward domestic vendors in order to develop domestic supercomputer and satellite industries.[18] In both cases, there was clear evidence that Japan was seeking to boost its industries in these sectors. Whether or not one accepts the premise that these industries are critical and deserve special emphasis, there is little debate that countering Japanese protectionism aimed at dominating an industry is important.

In both cases, agreements to reform Japanese procurement practices were reached. Cray Research, Inc., the U.S. supercomputer vendor, has successfully sold supercomputers to the Japanese government, though results have varied from year to year and Cray's market share in the Japanese governmental market lags behind its worldwide share. In response to continuing problems and as a result of concerns over Japanese compliance, the U.S. Trade Representative's office initiated a review in 1993. In this review, the United States gained some additional assurances from Japan, and more U.S. supercomputers were sold.

A similar story exists in the satellite case, but with two important differences. First, the size of the Japanese satellite market is quite small.[19] Second, the U.S. industry has been a less active supporter of this trade action than of the other two trade actions. Here again, if the agreement is to succeed in boosting U.S. sales, continuing efforts will be required by both the industry and the U.S. government.

Brazilian Import Licenses, 1989

Although Brazil was not widely seen as a likely candidate for action under Super 301, it certainly deserved identification. At the time it was identified, Brazil maintained a web of formal trade barriers, including tariffs, import quotas, and standard and testing requirements rivaling those of any other country. Import licenses—the particular barrier identified—are government licenses required before a product can be imported. They amount to government-managed quotas on all products. Thus, in scope, the Brazilian import licenses case corresponded more closely to the original intent of the authors of Super 301 than any of the other cases initiated in 1989.[20]

There can be no argument as to the outcome of the case. The United States successfully concluded an agreement with Brazil to end its policy of import licensing. Substantial progress toward market liberalization was also made with Brazil. This would seem to be an overwhelming victory for Super 301, and indeed it is. But some critics choose to deny Super 301 the credit in this instance, arguing that it was political change in Brazil, and not Super 301, that resulted in Brazil's adopting a more market-oriented economic posture. Unquestionably, there was a dramatic political change in Brazil. The election of President Ferdinand Collor de Mello in December of 1989 fundamentally altered the direction of Brazil's economic policy and made an agreement far more likely. It is a fallacy, however, to separate so strictly political and economic events. The looming trade conflict with the United States could have contributed to shifting political events in Brazil in a number of ways—e.g., encouraging support for President Collor. Most of the commentators evaluating this case—including the author—do not qualify as experts on Brazilian politics. Nonetheless, it is at least a surprising coincidence that, just at the moment that Brazil's economic policies were about to spark a trade conflict with the United States, a fundamental shift occurred in Brazilian politics to change those policies.[21] It is also notable that one of the first steps taken by the new Collor government was to resolve the dispute with the United States.

It would be presumptuous to conclude that Super 301 by itself caused a fundamental shift in Brazilian politics. By their nature, elections reflect the judgments of individuals, each of whom has an agenda. It is, however, at least as presumptuous to declare the events entirely disconnected. Government motivations in all trade negotiations, and particularly those involving Section 301, are difficult to define, but the threat of sanctions under Section 301 is certainly one of the considerations.

Indian Insurance and Investment, 1989

As with Brazil, the selection of India as a Super 301 priority foreign country came as a surprise, but India also richly deserved designation. At the time, India practiced and continues to practice (though substantial reforms have been undertaken) sweeping protectionism throughout its economy. Insurance and investment are examples of sectors in which India maintains substantial and obvious trade barriers.[22]

Negotiations with India would have been difficult under the best of circumstances given the strong nationalistic tendencies in Indian trade policy. India refused to negotiate under Super 301, arguing that the statute violated the GATT. The negotiations might have been more successful, however, if the Bush administration had taken a harder line. As it was, USTR Carla Hills merely issued a press release after twelve months—the statutory length of the cases—indicating that the negotiations had not been successful and that the Bush administration had declined to retaliate, preferring to continue negotiating in the Uruguay Round.[23] If, in fact, the cases with India were among the highest trade priorities of the United States, as the statute stipulates, it is difficult to understand why the Bush administration so quietly dropped the matter—particularly since, at the time, Indian goods were still eligible for preferential tariff treatment under the Generalized System of Preferences (GSP) program.[24] Of course, one can only speculate how the cases might have proceeded with vigorous enforcement, but it is hard to imagine that a more aggressive approach would have accomplished less.

The Most Productive Month in Trade Negotiation History

In 1989, Ambassador Carla Hills commented on negotiation activities during the month between the release of the National Trade Estimate—which serves as a warning of likely identification under Super 301—and the actual announcement of Super 301 priorities by saying, "We have probably had more intense negotiations over the past 30 days than we could have achieved without the law... Some countries really do not wish to be designated. We have gotten good and productive negotiations in this very short window."[25] She pointed out that a number of countries, including Korea and Taiwan, were willing to make concessions to the United States to avoid being identified under Super 301.

The Korean and Taiwanese agreements are particularly noteworthy because both promised a series of tariff cuts and other actions to reduce the U.S. trade deficit with these countries. Korea also agreed to increased transparency in its trade policy-making regime and increased investment liberalization.[26] These agreements did not address every American trade complaint with the two countries, however, and Korea and Taiwan both leave much to be desired in their enforcement of intellectual property rights. Korea also adopted a more protectionist policy stance in 1991 and 1992,[27] after Super 301 had been allowed to lapse. Both of the agreements made to forestall action under Super 301 were positive steps for American trade policy, but enforcement and followup are the keys to making these trade agreements meaningful.

Ambassador Hills's description of the one-month period between the NTE and Super 301 priority announcements led to a number of legislative proposals to extend Super 301, as well as to extend the period between the release of the NTE and the Super 301 announcements from one to six months.[28] The Clinton administration ultimately adopted this feature in its formulation of Super 301 by Executive Order. The Clinton administration recognizes the importance of Super 301, but there is not much evidence that it has used Super 301 leverage as vigorously as it might. In 1995, however, it did use the period leading up to the September Super 301 announcement to conclude an agreement with Korea aimed at opening the Korean auto market.

Notes

1. Office of the President, "Identification of Trade Expansion Priorities Executive Order" (press release), March 3, 1994.

2. See "China Market Access, 1991," p. 21.

3. Stuart Auerbach, "Japan Off U.S. Unfair Trader List; India Singled Out for Possible Retaliation," *Washington Post*, April 28, 1990, D10.

4. Peter Truell, "U.S. Won't Name More 'Unfair Traders,' Sparking Some Criticism from Congress," *Wall Street Journal*, April 30, 1990, A3.

5. Martin Crutsinger, "U.S., Japan Reach Deals, Heading Off Trade War," *Commercial Appeal*, October 2, 1994.

6. Bob Davis, "Economy: Japanese and U.S. Business Groups Propose Plan to Resolve Trade Tensions," *Wall Street Journal*, June 24, 1994, A2; Peter Behr, "As Trade Triumphs Fade, Clinton Faces Series of Tough Fights," *Washington Post*, May 14, 1994, C1.

7. Office of the USTR, "Super 301 Transmitted to Congress by USTR," "President Extends Super 301 by Executive Order," "USTR Kantor announces Agreement with Korea on Autos," (press releases), September 28, 1995.

8. Office of the USTR, *1990 National Trade Estimate Report on Foreign Trade Barriers* (Washington, DC: USTR), 107; Labor/Industry Coalition for International Trade, *Opening Japan: Recommendations for a Real World Solution* (Washington, DC: LICIT, September 1994), 29–34.

9. Office of the Press Secretary, White House, "Statement by the President (on Super 301 priority practices and countries)," May 26, 1989.

10. The term "adversarial trade" was in Title III of the Senate version of the Trade Act of 1987 (not passed) and was used by Peter Drucker to describe Japan: "Japan practices 'adversarial trade,' which changes the basic rules of fair trade. The aim of adversarial trade is to drive a competitor out of the market altogether rather

42   Section 301 Laws

than let it survive" (Stuart Auerbach, "Global Stakes High as Decision on Japan Trade Nears," *Washington Post*, May 25, 1989, C12).

11. Hobart Rowen, "Hills Optimistic About Japanese Cooperation; Paris OECD Talks to Begin Amid Uncertainty on Trade Issue," *Washington Post*, May 31, 1989, F4.

12. Stuart Auerbach, "The Scramble To Stay Clear of 'Super 301'; Foreign Producers Fear U.S. Trade List," *Washington Post*, April 11, 1989, E1.

13. International Trade Administration, U.S. Department of Commerce, *The Japanese Solid Wood Products Market* (Washington, DC: DOC, 1989), 174–77.

14. Japanese wood products case history from: Office of the USTR, *Report to Congress on Section 301 Developments Required by Section 309 (a) (3) of the Trade Act of 1974*, January-December 1993; International Trade Administration, U.S. Department of Commerce, *The Japanese Solid Wood Products Market* (Washington, DC: DOC, 1989).

15. International Trade Administration, U.S. Department of Commerce, *The Japanese Solid Wood Products Market* (Washington, DC: DOC, 1989).

16. Office of the USTR, *Report to Congress on Section 301 Developments Required by Section 309 (a) (3) of the Trade Act of 1974*, January-December 1993, 29.

17. A recent article in the *New York Times* cited continuing protectionism in this area, specifically in a recent requirement that the bidders for building the skating rink for the Winter Olympics use a wood grown only in Japan; see Sheryl WuDunn, "U.S. Companies Slip on Way to Winter Olympics," *New York Times*, March 20, 1995, A4.

18. Japanese supercomputer and satellite case histories from: Office of the USTR, *Report to Congress on Section 301 Developments Required by Section 309 (a) (3) of the Trade Act of 1974* January-December 1993; Office of the USTR, *1994 National Trade Estimate Report on Foreign Trade Barriers* (Washington, DC: USTR, 1994), 157–58.

19. Office of the USTR, *1994 National Trade Estimate on Foreign Trade Barriers* (Washington, DC: USTR, 1994), 157.

20. Brazilian import license case history from: Office of the USTR, *1990 National Trade Estimate on Foreign Trade Barriers* (Washington, DC: USTR, 1990), 15–17; Office of the Press Secretary, White House, "Statement by the President (on Super 301 priority practices and countries)," May 26, 1989.

21. William R. Long, "Brazil's President Moving Swiftly to Stimulate, Transform Country—Latin America: Bold Steps of the Last Six Months are Stirring Excitement and Uncertainty," *Los Angeles Times*, September 29, 1990, 16.

22. Indian insurance case history from: Office of the USTR, *1990 National Trade Estimate on Foreign Trade Barriers* (Washington, DC: USTR, 1990), 87–93; Office of the Press Secretary, White House, "Statement by the President (on Super 301 priority practices and countries)," May 26, 1989.

23. Stuart Auerbach, "U.S. Won't Retaliate Against India on Trade," *Washington Post,* June 14, 1990, C1.

24. This status was later curtailed in a dispute over intellectual property.

25. Stuart Auerbach, "Hills: Threat of Unfair Trade List Effective; Countries Now More Willing to Negotiate with U.S. on Barriers," *Washington Post*, May 13, 1989, D12.

26. Stuart Auerbach, "Japan Cited by Bush as Unfair Trader; Brazil, India on List: Tokyo 'Disappointed,'" *Washington Post*, May 26, 1989, A1; Stuart Auerbach, "U.S. Eyes Three Nations for Unfair Trading; Japan, India and Brazil May Be Cited," *Washington Post,* May 20, 1989, D11.

27. Office of the USTR, *1994 National Trade Estimate on Foreign Trade Barriers* (Washington, DC: USTR, 1994), 185–96.

28. Stuart Auerbach, "Democrats Seek To Extend Tough Trade Law; Measure Allows Sanctions Against Nations That Don't Drop Barriers," *Washington Post*, November 5, 1991, D1.

Chapter Six

The Record of Special 301

For all the controversy surrounding the one-year operational life of Super 301, its close cousin, Special 301, has gotten comparatively little attention. More Section 301 cases have been initiated under Special 301 than under Super 301, more countries have been the target of action under Special 301 than Super 301, and the cases initiated under Special 301 have been among the largest Section 301 cases. In sum, Special 301 can be fairly credited with improving respect for intellectual property in at least twenty countries and for helping to conclude the Uruguay Round negotiations on intellectual property—a significant set of achievements for a virtually unnoticed trade statute.[1] See Table 6.1.

Table 6.1 **Special 301 Announcements, 1989–95**

YEAR	1989	1990	1991	1992	1993[1]	1994[2]	1995
Priority Foreign Country	NONE	NONE	India China Thailand	India Thailand Taiwan	India Thailand Brazil	India China Argentina	

Table 6.1 (continued)

YEAR	1989	1990	1991	1992	1993[1]	1994[2]	1995
Priority Watch List	Brazil India Mexico China Korea Saudi Arabia Taiwan Thailand	Brazil India China Thailand	Brazil Australia EC	Brazil Australia EC Korea	Argentina Taiwan[3] Australia EC Korea Saudi Arabia Egypt Hungary Philippines Poland Turkey	Japan Thailand[4] EU (EC) Korea Saudi Arabia Egypt Hungary Poland Turkey	Brazil India EU Greece Saudi Arabia Japan Korea Turkey
Watch List	Argentina Canada Chile Colombia Egypt Greece Indonesia Italy Japan Malaysia Pakistan Philippines Portugal Spain Turkey Venezuela Yugoslavia	Argentina Canada Chile Colombia Egypt Greece Indonesia Italy Japan Malaysia Pakistan Philippines Spain Turkey Venezuela Yugoslavia Korea Saudi Arabia[5] Taiwan[6]	Argentina Canada Chile Colombia Egypt Greece Indonesia Italy Japan Pakistan Philippines Spain Turkey Venezuela Yugoslavia Korea Saudi Arabia Taiwan Cyprus Germany Hungary New Zealand United Arab Emirates	Argentina Canada Chile Colombia Greece Indonesia Italy Japan Pakistan Spain Venezuela Saudi Arabia Cyprus Germany New Zealand United Arab Emirates China[7] Ecuador El Salvador Guatemala Paraguay Peru	Chile Colombia Greece Indonesia Italy Japan Pakistan Philippines[8] Spain Venezuela Cyprus United Arab Emirates China Ecuador El Salvador Guatemala Peru	Australia Chile Colombia Egypt[9] Greece Indonesia Italy Pakistan Philippines Spain Venezuela Taiwan[10] Cyprus United Arab Emirates El Salvador Guatemala Peru	Argentina Bahrain Canada Chile China Colombia Costa Rica Egypt Indonesia Italy Pakistan Philippines Poland Romania Russian Federation Singapore South Africa Taiwan Thailand United Arab Emerates Venezuela El Salvador Guatemala Peru
Special Mention [11]						Brazil[12] Canada Germany Honduras Israel Panama Paraguay Russia Singapore	Bulgaria Cyprus Germany Honduras Israel Jordan Kuwait Oman Paraguay Qatar Vietnam
Removed From Lists		Mexico[13]	Malaysia[14]	Turkey Yugoslavia	Canada[15] Germany New Zealand[16] Paraguay	Ecuador[17] Poland[18]	Australia Panama Spain

Source: Press releases and fact sheets from the Office of the USTR on Special 301, 1989–95.

Notes to Table 6.1

1	Ambassador Kantor instituted a new policy for out-of-cycle reviews in 1993 that allowed for Special 301 actions to be taken at any time during the year. The following actions were taken: • **Greece** was moved to the priority watch list in November 1994 for TV copyright piracy and maintained this designation in April 1995. • **Brazil** was moved to the priority watch list in April 1995 due to its failure to enact new patent, copyright, and computer software legislation. • Despite progress, **Saudi Arabia** remains on the priority watch list for high levels of computer software piracy. • **United Arab Emirates** will remain on the watch list for software, audio, and video piracy despite progress made. • **South Africa** is scheduled for an out-of-cycle review for completion in September 1996, for U.S. trademark concerns.
2	**India, China, and Argentina** were not officially named priority foreign countries, although all were made PFCs shortly after 1994 announcement.
3	**Taiwan** became an Immediate Action Plan Country under a new USTR policy. Taiwan approved a bilateral agreement on copyrighted materials and also passed a law to protect trade secrets.
4	**Thailand** passed a law to strengthen intellectual property protections, with additional protections for pharmaceuticals.
5	**Saudi Arabia** implemented a new copyright law.
6	**Taiwan** imposed stronger enforcement against piracy of U.S. movies and agreed to stronger copyright protection.
7	**China** and the United States signed a Memorandum of Understanding for better protection of U.S. intellectual property.
8	**The Philippines**, in 1993, signed an agreement with the United States on intellectual property.
9	**Egypt** passed a law establishing a 50-year term for copyrighted computer software.
10	**Taiwan** passed a law against pirated television programs, and additional intellectual property laws were passed.
11	This is a new category added in 1994 by the USTR.
12	**Brazil,** subject to a Section 301 investigation, outlined plans for better intellectual property protections.
13	**Mexico** published comprehensive plans to modernize intellectual property protections and strengthened enforcement against piracy.
14	**Malaysia** accepted the Berne Convention for the Protection of Literary and Artistic Works guidelines and strengthened enforcement of copyright laws.
15	The **Canadian** legislature passed a law ending compulsory licensing for pharmaceutical products.
16	**New Zealand** repealed a compulsory licensing law for pharmaceuticals.
17	**Ecuador** signed a comprehensive intellectual property agreement with the United States.
18	**Poland** enacted a new law for copyright protections.

Special 301 has an interesting history. It was included in the 1988 Trade Act and largely modeled on Super 301. It differs from Super 301 in one important way: It is a permanent law with no expiration date, whereas Super 301 was to expire after two years. The deadlines for action under Super 301 and Special 301 were originally the same, April 30. As a result, in 1989 and 1990, Special 301 received little attention, being overshadowed by Super 301. The Bush administration—never an anxious user of Section 301 and feeling no congressional or public pressure to use Special 301—declined to initiate cases under the statute.

The Bush administration did, however, devise a system of "watch lists" in conjunction with Special 301. In lieu of actually initiating cases, the administration put countries on a "watch list" and a "priority watch list," signifying that the United States objected to the status of intellectual property protection in those countries. Listing on the priority watch list indicated that the country might be identified in the future under Special 301 as a "priority foreign country" and be subject to a Section 301 investigation. (To add to the complexity, some countries were mentioned in the annual press release on Special 301 action but not actually placed on a watch list, thus creating a fourth tier of scrutiny.) The watch lists were unquestionably devised, at least in part, to avoid action under Special 301, but perhaps to everyone's surprise they worked well. A number of countries, including Mexico, Australia, Ecuador, and Germany, took action largely to be removed from or downgraded on the watch lists.

By 1991, however, Super 301 had expired and congressional and industry pressure had built for action under Special 301. Cases were initiated against India, China, and Thailand. New cases were launched in each subsequent year to the present, and a number of those cases were successful. The cases against China are worthy of particular note. China was a priority foreign country in 1991. An agreement was negotiated with China in early 1992 under which it agreed to make a series of changes in Chinese laws to upgrade the overall strength of its intellectual property statutes to a very high level—among the highest in the world. Unfortunately, China neglected to enforce those laws, and the piracy of intellectual property continued largely unchecked.

A Special 301 case was initiated in 1994 that focused on enforcement of the 1992 commitments. On the last day before more than $1 billion in trade sanctions would have gone into effect, February 26, 1995, China agreed to a new enforcement regime and sanctions were suspended.[2] In late 1995 and 1996, however, strong evidence came to light that China had failed to enforce this agreement. In early April 1996, intense negotiations are under way to improve enforcement. If the current negotiations fail, the United States has threatened to impose up to two billion dollars in sanctions. Cases were also initiated against Thailand, Taiwan, Brazil, and Argentina. Some of these countries have yet to make the promised changes in law, however, and could be possible future candidates for action under Special 301.

Special 301 has piled up a record of achievement rivaling that of any other trade statute. It is fair to say that Special 301—with the addition of its watch lists—worked more like Super 301 was intended to work than Super 301 ever did. As noted, Special 301 has won improved market access or intellectual property protection in more than twenty countries through the initiation of cases and watch list warnings. The success of Special 301 is very strong evidence that a market-opening strategy built around consistent, aggressive, and creative use of Section 301 can be very effective while avoiding the pitfalls cited by critics. If Super 301 had received the same permanent status and the same creative application, perhaps it would have amassed a similarly successful record.

Notes

1. Press releases and fact sheets, Office of the USTR on Special 301, 1989–94.
2. Early evidence indicates that China has made some efforts to stop illegal street-level retailing, but regardless, illegal reproduction of intellectual property seems to continue unabated.

Chapter Seven

The Case for Extending Super 301 and Special 301

As noted, Super 301 and Special 301 have been under criticism from the outset. One recent study came to the conclusion that Super 301 is "unnecessary and undesirable." The essence of the argument was that Super 301 is unpopular with our trading partners and that normal Section 301 cases are as effective as Super 301 cases.[1] This analysis simply ignores the rationale for Super 301: to set American trade priorities and to initiate Section 301 cases in support of those priorities.[2]

Initiating Cases

Congress drafted Super 301 to force the executive branch to initiate Section 301 cases. Congress believed that the executive branch was unwilling to initiate cases against major trading partners for fear of ruffling diplomatic feathers.[3] It seems there is an almost endless list of foreign elections, military base negotiations, and other diplomatic considerations whenever a major trade action is being contemplated, and regardless of the administration in office, there are always strong voices arguing that the time is not right.

These voices are remarkably effective. Those who foretell a fundamental shift in American foreign policy away from diplomatic and security objectives to economic ones greatly underestimate the bureaucratic strength of agencies such as the State Department, the National Security Council, and the Treasury Department. These agencies, fearful of disrupting diplomatic objectives, security concerns, and international economic coordination, maintain strong institutional interests against an aggressive trade policy. The office of the U.S. Trade Representative clearly has growing influence, but it still cannot compete with these bureaucratic giants on an even footing.

Thus, it is no surprise that all but a handful of the cases that have been self-initiated by the U.S. government in the last six years have been forced, directly or indirectly, by Super 301 or Special 301. Most cases that were self-initiated outside of Special 301 and Super 301—including one against China (discussed previously) and one against Canada after public refutation of a previously reached trade agreement—were unique. Recent history makes one fact overwhelmingly clear: Barring a major change in the bureaucratic culture, without Super 301 and Special 301, major trade actions simply will not be initiated by any administration.

It is true that many Section 301 cases have been initiated by petition from domestic industries. Petition initiating is an important feature of Section 301, but the authors of the statute realized early that the threat of retaliation by foreign governments often keeps private companies from initiating action. Private companies are very vulnerable to subtle retaliation in the enforcement of regulations or the letting of contracts and sometimes prefer to suffer protectionism rather than risk retaliation that might make matters worse. In those cases—which seem more the rule than the exception—the U.S. government, and only the U.S. government, can act.

Super 301 performs the essential function of requiring an annual listing of priorities and initiation of Section 301 cases. History—indeed, quite recent history—indicates that if action-forcing deadlines are not institutionalized in law, action will not be taken. If Super 301 and Special 301 were not in the law, the self-initiation of cases would become the rarely used alternative it was before the mid-1980s. Section 301—the most effective tool for opening foreign markets—would be used only rarely, and not against powerful trading partners. And since the private sector is hesitant to challenge foreign governments on its own, foreign governments would be seldom challenged at all.

Deterrent Effect

The annual cycle of Super 301 also has a positive deterrent effect on foreign countries. Major trading partners know that a reversion to protectionism will run the risk of U.S. action under Super 301. Without the annual review, U.S. trading partners—who are quite familiar with the U.S. political system—understand all too well that action beyond rhetoric is unlikely. As mentioned previously, many observers found it more than coincidental that Korea's reversion to open protectionism occurred just after Super 301 was allowed to lapse.[4]

The deterrent effect is even clearer under Special 301. The watch and priority watch lists provide a dual function: warning of future action, and creating a forum to focus attention on foreign efforts to fulfill promises made. The long list of countries that have reformed their intellectual property laws merely to be removed from the watch lists is a strong testament to the operation of the deterrent effect. Since Special 301 is a permanent feature of U.S. trade law, trading partners are on constant notice that a reversion to piracy of U.S. intellectual property will bring future trade action. Special 301's annual reviews can continue to perform the essential function as the focus broadens to include enforcement of new WTO intellectual property provisions.

The ramifications for both market access and protection of intellectual property are clear. The understanding that the United States will be reviewing its trade situation with a determined regularity will put piracy-minded and protectionist countries on notice that Section 301 action is always a possibility.

Notes

1. Thomas O. Bayard and Kimberly Ann Elliot, "Reciprocity and Retaliation," in *U.S. Trade Policy* (Washington, DC: Institute for International Economics, 1994) 313–22.

2. The difference between Section 301 and Super 301 is that Super 301 requires the USTR to identify and initiate investigations against countries with trade barriers, whereas, Section 301 simply allows the USTR the right to investigate cases.

3. Stuart Auerbach, "U.S. Weighs Trade Move Against Japan," *Washington Post*, March 28, 1984, 7.

4. Damon Darlin, "Closing Door: South Korea Regresses on Opening Markets, Trade Partners Say," *Wall Street Journal,* June 12, 1990, A1.

Chapter Eight

Refutation of Major Criticisms

Protectionism

The criticism most frequently aimed at Section 301—particularly Super 301—has been that it is a device for protectionism. This is a peculiar charge given that the aim of Section 301 is to open markets, not to close them. Apparently, protectionism, like beauty, is in the eye of the beholder.

The claim critics appear to be making, though they rarely state it, is that the threat of raising tariffs to block imports in retaliation for foreign trade barriers is an excuse for protectionism. In actual experience, a Section 301 case normally takes at least a year to reach the point where retaliation is seriously contemplated. During this period, the United States engages in extensive negotiations with the foreign governments involved to remove the trade barriers in question. As Linn Williams, deputy USTR for the Bush administration remarked, "If the U.S. wanted to close markets, we would have done it differently."[1] Further, the goal of sanctions is to spur action on the part of the foreign government involved, not to protect the U.S. sector involved in the Section 301 case. Once a decision to retaliate is reached, retaliation is normally taken in a sector quite removed from the issue involved in the Section 301 case. Thus, the industry involved is very unlikely to pursue a Section 301 case as a means of raising trade barriers to protect itself.

Aggressive Unilateralism

A more sophisticated criticism frequently raised against Section 301 is that it amounts to "aggressive unilateralism." As noted at the outset, these critics characterize Section 301 as the United States' attempt to act as "judge, jury, and executioner" in trade disputes that would be better handled multilaterally through the GATT, or now, presumably, the WTO. The authors of a recent book on Section 301 suggest that "aggressive unilateralism" be replaced with "aggressive multilateralism," meaning to work through the WTO instead of Section 301.[2]

Many of the critics and commentators have apparently not studied the legislative history of the statute. Section 301 was designed from the outset to work with the multilateral trade dispute settlement process. In fact, the United States used the time lines for action under Section 301 to negotiate the dispute settlement time limits in the Uruguay Round Agreement. As noted, in the legislation to implement the Uruguay Round, the time limits for action under Section 301 were further refined to assure complete conformance with the multilateral trade dispute settlement process. Section 301 actually *requires* the president to pursue consultations through the multilateral trade dispute settlement process in those Section 301 cases involving violations of the WTO.[3] Further, if the dispute settlement panel rules against the U.S. position, the president can decline to retaliate on that basis alone. In short, "aggressive multilateralism" merely describes the way Section 301 is designed to operate.

A problem arises in those cases in which the issues involved are not covered by a trade agreement with an adequate dispute settlement procedure. Before the Uruguay Round, many issues—including agriculture, services, and intellectual property—were not effectively covered in a multilateral trade agreement. Partially as a result, many of the Section 301 cases pursued in the last decade were pursued outside the GATT because the issues central to the case could not be pursued through the GATT. The Uruguay Round Agreement greatly expanded the scope of issues covered by multilateral agreement; agriculture, services, and intellectual property are to greater and lesser extents now covered. As a result, a greater percentage of future Section 301 cases are likely to be pursued in close coordination with multilateral trade dispute settlement because such coordination is possible.

There will still be cases that cannot be pursued through multilateral institutions, either because the target country involved is not a party to the new WTO or because the issue to be addressed is not covered by the WTO. A number of major trading countries remain outside the WTO and are likely to remain so for some time. Trade problems that are increasingly recognized as serious commercial problems, including private-sector collusion and forced technology transfer, are also beyond the scope of the WTO. In these cases, the United States will be faced with a simple choice: either act unilaterally or be prepared to tolerate the unfair practice. In those cases in which a multilateral "judge and jury" is simply unavailable, unilateral action under Section 301 remains the only solution.

Trade War

A final criticism frequently leveled against Section 301 is that it risks prompting a major trade war. Part of the confusion surrounding this argument is the imprecise definition of the term "trade war." If the critics mean that the United States may impose retaliatory tariffs on a targeted list of products and the foreign country involved will threaten similar action, they may well be correct. Many countries, when faced with United States retaliation, normally threaten counter-retaliation. This is the routine course of action in disputes with China and the European Union.[4]

This type of trade war is not necessarily bad. Three factors should be kept in mind. First, in every case in which the United States has threatened to retaliate or actually retaliated, it acted in the face of foreign trade barriers that were costing U.S. exporters hundreds of millions and sometimes billions of dollars each year after it had exhausted other options for resolving the dispute.[5] Second, the application of sanctions is often a catalyst for reaching an agreement to resolve the dispute. For example, in the three recent disputes with China previously discussed, retaliation and counter-retaliation were threatened in each case, and an agreement to resolve the dispute was reached only in the face of imminent retaliation. It appears that several major U.S. trading partners, including Japan and China, have difficulty reaching a political consensus to act until the adverse consequences of further foot-dragging are apparent. In fact, as the reader can see in Table 4.1, the threat, or actual application, of sanctions normally results in the resolution of the conflict, not the long-term application of sanctions and counter sanctions.

Finally—as the listing of Section 301 cases in Appendix A again demonstrates—sanctions, when applied, have always remained carefully targeted and focused. There is not a single example of a trade dispute escalating into a major trade war. When most critics use the term "trade war" as a criticism of Section 301, they seem to be raising the specter of a widespread effort to raise trade barriers similar to what occurred at the outset of the Great Depression. The actual sequence of events related to the raising of tariffs at the outset of the Great Depression, and their contribution to the global economic downturn, is open to considerable debate among historians and economists. In the post-Depression era, however, certain facts are clear. There have been no escalating cycles of retaliation and counter-retaliation. The examples that are cited, such as the so-called Chicken War between the United States and Europe, involved only very small trade volumes compared to the total, and Section 301 cannot be cited as the cause of the Chicken War.[6] The closest parallel would be a round of sanctions and counter sanctions imposed by the United States and Europe in 1989 in a dispute over Europe's decision to block American beef exports; the total volume of sanctions in that dispute amounted to only about $200 million, or less than one-eighth of 1 percent of total U.S.-European trade.[7]

One of the realities of economic globalization is that a trade war is only a shade more rational than a nuclear war, harder to launch, and nearly as unpalatable. In most sectors—in the United States, Europe, and Japan—there is a high volume of intra-industry trade. Almost without exception, manufacturing companies in all countries rely on imports for components and/or export a significant percentage of their annual production. These same facts are often incorrectly cited as reasons the United States should simply ignore foreign trade barriers. That makes little sense, because, as the previous discussion in this volume makes clear, significant trade barriers and unfair trade practices remain and impose a cost on the U.S. economy. To ignore trade barriers that block additional billions of dollars in U.S. exports because the United States already exports some billions of dollars' worth of products doesn't follow. However, the significant economic relationship does make it extremely unlikely that any major economic power would engage in a widespread trade war since its own economic interests would be an early casualty of such a conflict.

Targeted sanctions, however, have been and continue to be an effective tool for spurring further market opening in U.S. trade partners. Further, for a variety of historical reasons, the United States voluntarily opened its market to trade more widely than many of its trading partners. The threat of sanctions is often the only practical approach to opening markets, since the United States has less to bargain away in reciprocal negotiations, and leading by example has not proven to be an effective strategy. Surely, the threat of sanctions under Section 301 must be used cautiously and judiciously, but trade sanctions can be threatened and employed without any real risk of sparking a widespread trade war.

Notes

1. Stuart Auerbach, "Hills Defends Aggressive Trade Policy; Better System Is Goal, U.S. Official Says," *Washington Post*, June 9, 1989, F2.

2. Thomas O. Bayard and Kimberly Ann Elliot, *Reciprocity and Retaliation in U.S. Trade Policy* (Washington, DC: Institute for International Economics, 1994), 329–51.

3. The Uruguay Round Agreements Act of 1994, Pub. L. 103-465, 108 Stat. 4938-4943.

4. See cases #11, 27–31, 54, 81, 86, 88, 92 in Appendix A.

5. See the Japan semiconductors case (#48), European oilseeds case (#63), Canadian beer case (#80), and European beef case (#62), in Appendix A.

6. The Chicken War between the United States and Europe took place in the 1960s; Section 301 was initially implemented in 1974.

7. Total U.S. trade (exports plus imports) with the European Union in 1989 was $171,716 million (U.S. Department of Commerce, *U.S. Foreign Trade Highlights*, Washington, DC, 1993).

Chapter Nine

Section 301 in the WTO Era

As discussed previously, the advent of the new world trading system will mean changes in the way Section 301 and its relatives, Super 301 and Special 301, are employed, but—to paraphrase Mark Twain—rumors of the death of Section 301 have been greatly exaggerated. As the Clinton administration's use of Section 301 in the auto and auto parts negotiations with Japan demonstrates, Section 301 remains an effective and flexible tool for pressing trade disputes. Section 301 can continue to play four very important roles in the new WTO world.

Section 301 and the WTO

In a very real sense, the WTO was in large part spawned by Section 301. The authors of Section 301, Super 301, and Special 301 were not only aware of multilateral trade negotiations, but, in fact, tailored their legislation to complement and support U.S. objectives in those negotiations. Senator John Danforth, a leading sponsor of the Omnibus Trade and Competitiveness Act of 1988, said during consideration of the conference report, "What we attempted to do in this legislation was to create some consistency in the enforcement of trade laws and the enforcement of international agreements." He later added, "Mandatory retaliation against trade agreement violations represents a fundamental change from current law, where Section 301 has been used. These new provisions put our trading partners on notice that we expect them to play by the rules of the game, that violation of our rights in the trade arena will no longer be tolerated."[1]

In a political sense, it was American use of Section 301 that convinced much of the rest of the world that a stronger, more reliable dispute settlement was an attractive alternative—especially since the United States could act on its own in the absence of such a dispute settlement mechanism. Further, as noted at several points, Section 301 is structured to reinforce the new WTO dispute settlement mechanism. The WTO dispute settlement process has the effect of "internationalizing Section 301" and adding the credibility of international dispute settlement to it.[2] Section 301 also provides the dispute settlement process with the backing of likely trade sanctions as well as international condemnation.

Section 301, or more precisely, Special 301 and Super 301, can focus U.S. efforts to employ WTO dispute settlement effectively. At their core, both Special 301 and Super 301 are formal processes for setting priorities; the original section of law authorizing Super 301 is titled "Identification of Trade Liberalization Priorities."[3] As previously mentioned, Super 301 mandates the creation of a list of foreign countries and trade barriers that block the largest quantities of U.S. exports. In close parallel, Special 301 generates an annual list of the countries that deny protection and market access to U.S. intellectual property. As the United States presses to eliminate practices and barriers that do not conform with the provisions of the new Uruguay Round Agreement, those priorities must again be identified. It is logical to employ the Super 301 and Special 301 listings as a priority list for action under the WTO. This logic is apparently not lost on some of the United States' trading partners. As noted, Europe is considering its own close analogue to Super 301 to focus and coordinate its efforts at WTO dispute settlement.

Finally, international dispute settlement procedures mean very little in isolation. The only sanction that can directly be applied by the WTO is international criticism or condemnation. The WTO can authorize the withdrawal of trade benefits (read: sanctions), but it does not make the decision to impose sanctions—that step is left to the national governments involved. As was clearly demonstrated in a number of cases examined previously, including the European oilseeds case and the Canadian beer case, winning a dispute settlement panel is often not enough to convince foreign governments to end trade barriers. The threat of sanctions is often necessary. Section 301, and the threat of trade sanctions that it carries, can thus be used to support multilateral trade dispute settlement by backing WTO decisions favorable to the United States. Just as its authors intended, Section 301 and multilateral trade dispute settlement can continue to work together in a mutually reinforcing manner. See Table 9.1.

Table 9.1 **Section 301 and World Trade Organization Dispute Settlement**

SECTION 301 ACTION	TIMELINE	WTO DSB ACTION
Petition filed	45 Days before initiation	
Initiation/self-initiation by USTR of 301 case.	5 Days before initiation	
Request for consultations for disputes not covered under trade agreements, ones involving the subsidy agreement or Intellectual Property, USTR begins bilateral consultations. For WTO-covered disputes, process at right begins.	Day 1 Day 1	**Request for consultations**
	Day 10	**Response due** from target country
	End of Month 1	**Consultations must begin**
	End of Month 2	**Consultations completed** if unsuccessful, petitioner requests panel formation.
	Month 3, Day 25	**Panel formed**
Latest date to request consultations.	End of Month 3	
	Month 4, Day 15	**Members of panel determined**
	End of Month 8	**Panel report due**
	Month 9, Day 20	**Decision to WTO** must be Adopted, Appealed or Unanimously Declined by WTO Council.
	Month 11, Day 20	**Appeal complete**
Determination due for disputes outside WTO.[a]	End of End of Month 12 Month 12	**Adoption by DSB**

60 Section 301 Laws

Table 9.1 (continued)

SECTION 301 ACTION	TIMELINE	WTO DSB ACTION
USTR must act in response to WTO decision.[b]	End of Month 13	
Latest date for action by USTR in disputes involving trade agreements.	End of Month 18	

WTO - World Trade Organization ◊ **DSB** - Dispute Settlement Body
a. Determination can be delayed additional three months if target country is making significant progress.
b. USTR must act 1 month after DSB decision, or 18 months after initiation of case, whichever is earlier.

Source: The Uruguay Round Agreements Act, Pub. L. 103-465, 108 Stat. 4938-4943.

In the mid-1980s, both the United States and Europe considered undertaking a group action under the GATT against Japan, alleging that Japan's informal trade barriers "nullified and impaired" concessions it had made under the GATT and should be declared violations of the GATT. There was also discussion in Congress of implementing Super 301 in this manner. This option was rejected because GATT dispute settlement procedures were weak. Now, with the improved WTO dispute settlement procedures, Super 301 could be used to launch action against Japan or other countries that maintain a web of informal trade barriers against imported products. This possibility has been actively discussed in regard to both of the most recent U.S. trade disputes involving autos and auto parts and photographic film.

Enforcing Trade Agreements

The United States is party to dozens of bilateral trade agreements outside of the GATT/WTO framework[4] (although all are consistent with the GATT/WTO). Many of these agreements have been the result of Section 301 cases; others are simply settlements of bilateral trade disputes. Just in the short history of the Clinton administration, fourteen such agreements have been concluded with Japan alone.[5]

Unfortunately, the United States has proven more adept at negotiating these agreements than it has been at enforcing them.

Complaints of serious foreign noncompliance with these agreements number well into the dozens—including Japanese noncompliance with the U.S.-Japan Semiconductor Agreement and the U.S.-Japan Supercomputer Agreement, Chinese noncompliance with both intellectual property and market access agreements, and Canadian noncompliance with the 1987 Softwood Lumber Memorandum of Understanding. These agreements all exist outside of the WTO, so that WTO dispute settlement is simply not an option in these cases. These bilateral agreements also lack adequate dispute settlement procedures of their own.

Section 301 was developed with special attention to such violations of bilateral agreements. The Section 301 statute contains a special provision for addressing violations of Section 301 agreements, Section 306. Further, the authors of Section 301 created special procedures for addressing violations of trade agreements on a swift and sure track. As the above examples make quite clear, violations of trade agreements are a continuing problem. With some countries, noncompliance seems to be the rule and not the exception.

Even if all future trade disputes could be handled exclusively through the WTO—an unlikely event indeed—Section 301 could perform a vital role for decades to come merely by enforcing the bilateral agreements that currently exist. In fact, the United States should be much more vigorously insisting on full compliance with agreements. The historic tendency of U.S. trade negotiators to declare victory once an agreement is reached and then go on to the next problem has severely undermined the credibility of U.S. trade policy. If an administration were to do nothing else but assign its trade negotiators the job of enforcing existing agreements under Section 301, it could achieve a great deal.[6]

Countries Outside the WTO

Though the GATT and now the WTO are commonly referred to as the world trading system, membership is not universal. In fact, the foreign countries with which the United States runs its second and third largest annual trade deficit—China and Taiwan respectively[7]—are not members of the WTO. Both of these countries have desired for some time to join the GATT and now the WTO, but a variety of economic and political barriers have kept them out. Both countries are now engaged in intensive negotiations with the major nations of the WTO and hope to join in 1996. Perhaps the negotiations will succeed and perhaps they will not. A number of other countries that have significant trade relationships with the United States, including Russia, the former Soviet republics, Saudi Arabia, and some Eastern European countries, are not members of the WTO. As is the case with China and Taiwan, most of these countries desire to join the WTO, but the prospects of this happening in the short term are limited. In all likelihood, significant U.S. trading partners will remain outside the world trading system for a number of years.[8]

Given that these countries are outside the WTO, the United States has no avenue for establishing a multilateral trading relationship with them. Bilateral negotiations—normally under the rubric of Section 301—are the only option. As noted in the analysis above, the United States has pursued significant and successful Section 301 negotiations with both China and Taiwan. Without Section 301, market access and the protection of intellectual property in these countries would not have progressed as far as they have. As Russia and other formerly communist countries attempt to expand their trading relationship with the United States, problems—many of them best addressed with Section 301—are certain to arise. Already, significant trade disputes have surfaced involving aluminum produced in Russia.[9] Section 301 remains a critical tool for handling trade relations with non-WTO members.

Practices Outside the WTO

Few would disagree with the proposition that Section 301 should be used to open markets in non-WTO countries. More difficult issues arise when the *country* involved in a particular dispute does belong to the WTO, but the *barrier or practice* is not addressed by the WTO. The WTO certainly has greater coverage than the GATT; significant progress has been made extending multilateral discipline to agriculture, services, and intellectual property. Other critical practices, such as export targeting, foreign corrupt practices (shorthand for practices like bribery, which is common in some countries), and collusion, are not covered by the WTO. This is significant because collusion—sometimes called private-sector protectionism—is probably the single most serious of the remaining trade barriers and has been at the core of the two most recent trade disputes with Japan.[10]

Just a decade ago, there was extensive international debate over the issue of the protection of intellectual property, and whether it was even an appropriate topic for international trade negotiations. Some prominent developing countries (not coincidentally, the same countries that were major pirates of intellectual property) argued that this issue was best addressed by the World Intellectual Property Organization, or WIPO, a body known only for hosting endless ineffectual debates on the topic. The United States forced protection of intellectual property onto the international trade agenda and won a significant agreement to protect intellectual property, largely through aggressive use of Special 301. The U.S. application of Special 301 convinced many pirating countries that they would be forced to address intellectual property protection one way or the other. Faced with this reality, they opted to negotiate an agreement in the Uruguay Round.[11]

As the intellectual property experience demonstrates, Section 301 can be a catalyst for bringing new issues into the WTO. It is a broad and flexible tool. It can be used to address foreign trade barriers or practices that "burden or restrict" U.S. commerce. The legislation authorizing Section 301 specifically defines export targeting and collusion within its scope, but any practice that meets the test of burdening or restricting U.S. commerce can also be addressed under Section 301.[12] If the United States hopes to push issues onto the agenda and win agreements to address them, rhetoric and persuasion will not be enough. Action speaks far louder than words, and Section 301 is the most obvious avenue for action. If the United States is serious about addressing unfair trade barriers like collusion and export targeting, it must begin targeting examples of these practices under Section 301.

A similar situation is faced with the issues covered by the WTO but covered inadequately—the best example again being the protection of intellectual property. Although the WTO is groundbreaking in that it covers intellectual property, its coverage is not adequate in all areas. There is, for example, no patent protection for products that are now in the pipeline (the term for products under development). There are also long phase ins for some countries; as a result, full protection for pharmaceuticals and chemicals, for example, may be denied for a decade.

Similarly, the WTO has limited coverage of another serious intellectual problem: compulsory licensing. Compulsory licensing is the practice under which a foreign government insists that a company wishing to sell an intellectual property product in that market license the use of its technology to a firm within the foreign country or to the foreign government itself. The WTO does take steps to combat compulsory licensing,[13] but several loopholes and weaknesses in the provision allow considerable use of compulsory licenses. Singapore, normally an advocate for free trade, actually passed a new compulsory licensing provision just before the WTO took effect to take advantage of the weaknesses in the WTO provision.[14]

Forced technology transfer is a variant of compulsory licensing in which the transfer of technology is informally required as a condition of sales or investment, without a formal written law or rule. This practice is used particularly in those countries where policy is dictated more by informal government policy than by a publicly available law or regulation. For obvious reasons, this practice is difficult even to detect, let alone combat, but according to anecdotal reports, it is quite common. China has gained a particular reputation for engaging in this practice. Reports of Chinese efforts to require technology transfer come from the automobile, aerospace, semiconductor, and computer industries. Obviously, the practice of forced technology transfer is identical in effect to compulsory licensing, but it is not directly covered by the WTO. This loophole could easily lead enterprising foreign governments to transform today's compulsory licenses to tomorrow's forced technology transfers.[15]

In the case of China at least, the U.S. government is already on strong ground to complain about the practice of forced technology transfer. In the MOU concluding the 1992 market-access Section 301 case discussed previously, China agreed not to "condition issuance of import licenses upon transfer of technology or meeting requirements related to investment in China...."[16] Accordingly, forced technology transfer could be pursued under Section 301 as a violation of the 1992 market-access MOU. This action could be either initiated by a U.S. private-sector interest (industry, union, etc.) or self-initiated by the U.S. government.

There are weaknesses in other portions of the WTO affecting investment, agriculture, and other issues. It is probably inevitable that the creativity of protectionists and pirates will continually stay one step ahead of international trade agreements. For the last decade, the United States has used the flexibility of Section 301 to keep pace with the new generation of protectionism and mercantilism fairly effectively. Section 301 can fill the gaps in the WTO and combat the new generation of protectionism. In fact, if it is not used in this way, it is difficult to see any incentive that protectionists and pirates will have to limit their new practices.

There have always been critics of the practice of using Section 301 to counter the cutting edge of protectionism—usually coming from the countries that engage in the practices, or their defenders. Rhetoric in favor of multilateralism can sound quite persuasive, but it ignores one indisputable reality of modern commerce. Protectionism and mercantilism are unlikely to be curbed unless its practitioners are given an incentive to reform their practices. It is certainly possible to begin negotiations and consultations on these issues, but without the threat of sanctions, it is a recipe for an endless negotiating marathon.

The WTO does, however, give the advocates of endless negotiation a new argument. If the United States were to pursue one of these issues and eventually impose trade retaliation, the foreign country subject to the sanction—if it be a WTO member—could challenge the retaliation as a violation of the WTO. Given that the tariffs raised in retaliation for the foreign barrier would be bound under the WTO, a dispute settlement panel—particularly if it chose to take a narrow view of the issue—could rule against the United States and the WTO could then authorize the foreign country to counter-retaliate against U.S. exports.

There are, however, three powerful opposing arguments. First, the United States could seek retaliatory measures not barred by the WTO. Possibilities include stripping foreign countries of preferential tariff treatment under the Generalized System of Preferences (GSP) or the Caribbean Basin Initiative (CBI), if they are beneficiaries of either program. There are also other possibilities for blocking imports through *sub rosa* means, e.g.: imposing difficult inspection standards, a technique the French have used in the past. In drafting the legislation to implement the WTO, the Congress endorsed some of these approaches and others to keep Section 301 vital.

Second, Washington could attack unfair trade barriers with Section 301 on the grounds that they have the effect of "nullifying and impairing" the benefits promised under the WTO. According to the nullification and impairment concept, if a country pledges to eliminate a trade barrier under the GATT/WTO and then raises a new, different barrier in its place, other countries may challenge the GATT/WTO consistency of the replacement barrier—even if it is not specifically barred under the GATT/WTO—because it renders the initial trade concession meaningless. Thus, if a country eliminates its tariff on widgets and later imposes a subsidy to domestic widget producers, in effect blocking imported widgets, the subsidy can be challenged as a violation of the GATT/WTO. A number of nullification and impairment actions were successful under the GATT, and a number of authorities have suggested broader use of nullification and impairment complaints in support of Section 301 objectives. The approach is certainly credible, but it is also uncertain.[17]

The nullification and impairment counterclaim approach may get an early test in the U.S.-Japan photographic film dispute (case #99). Eastman Kodak, a U.S. corporation, alleged in its Section 301 filing that its Japanese competitor, Fuji Film, had been allowed and even encouraged by the Japanese government to collude with retailers to exclude Kodak film from Japan. If so, the U.S. could assert that Japan's toleration of collusion in its market nullifies and impairs numerous tariff concessions on film granted over the years and is thus a violation of the WTO. If successful, such a challenge would open the door to a long list of similar complaints in other sectors.[18]

Finally, it is important to recognize that the threat of counter-retaliation against Section 301 sanctioned by the WTO is not an entirely new prospect. GATT dispute settlement panels were likely to rule against U.S. retaliation on the same basis. In fact, the United States faced just such a dispute with Mexico when it retaliated against Mexico for its tuna fishing practices.[19] It is true that the United States could have chosen unilaterally to block the GATT from approving the panel's decision—an option now foreclosed by the WTO. The United States, however, did not choose to protect itself from GATT condemnation by blocking the decision in the dispute with Mexico, or in any other recent instances of the United States losing a dispute settlement panel. Since the United States has always been an advocate of strong international trade dispute settlement, it is very difficult for it to block dispute settlement unilaterally. In addition, a number of trading powers, including the EU and China, showed a willingness to counter-retaliate without international approval. In sum, though the WTO may make international criticism of U.S. action more likely, counter-retaliation is probably no more likely than it was in the past. Many countries will be reluctant to escalate a trade dispute with the United States under any circumstances.

In the end, the WTO does not fundamentally change the choice faced by future administrations; the choice is either to risk counter-retaliation or to tolerate protectionism and piracy. Section 301, backed with the market power of the United States, is a powerful tool for opening markets and winning protection for intellectual property. As previously stated, it is the only realistic tool to combat the next generation of protectionism and mercantilism. Section 301 can be effective in the new WTO trading system just as it was in the GATT system. Whether it is used comes down to a question of the priorities and courage of the U.S. government. Simply put, abandoning Section 301 means accepting protectionism.

Notes

1. U.S. Senate floor debate, April 22 and April 25, 1988.
2. Judith H. Bello and Alan Holmer, "GATT Dispute Settlement Agreement: Internationalization or Elimination of Section 301," *International Lawyer*, Fall, vol. 26, 1990.
3. United States Statutes at Large, 1974, vol. 88, part 2, and vol. 102, part 2.
4. Hearings before the Subcommittee on International Trade of the U.S. Senate Committee of Finance, July 13, 1990, on S. 2742, Trade Agreements Compliance Act.
5. Mention of the fourteen agreements was made in a speech by Ambassador Michael Kantor at the 1995 Economic Strategy Institute / Pacific Basin Economic Council–U.S. trade conference, "Winning and Losing: America in the New Global Trade Order," March 30, 1995.
6. The Clinton administration recently announced a new task force focusing on enforcement of existing trade agreements.
7. Department of Commerce, *U.S. Foreign Trade Highlights* (Washington, DC: DOC, 1993).
8. Greg Mastel, *Trading with the Middle Kingdom* (Washington, DC: Economic Strategy Institute, September 1995).

9. Erle Norton and Martin Du Bois, "Foiled Competition: Don't Call It a Cartel, But World Aluminum Has Forged New Order," *Wall Street Journal*, June 9, 1994, 1.

10. Coalition for Open Trade, *Dealing with Japan, Responding to Private Practices in Restraint of Trade: An Assessment of Policy Tools* (Washington, DC: COT, March 1994).

11. Monique L. Cordray, "GATT v. WIPO," *Journal of the Patent and Trademark Office Society*, February 1994, vol. 70:121; R. Michael Cadbaw, "Intellectual Property and International Trade: Merger or Marriage of Convenience?" *Vanderbilt Journal of Transnational Law*, Spring 1989, vol. 22:223.

12. Trade Act of 1974, Pub. L. 93-618, § 88 Stat. 2041 (1975).

13. The Uruguay Round Agreements Act of 1994, Pub. L. 103-465, 108 Stat. 4938-4943.

14. "U.S. PhRMA Seeks 'Special 301' Listings," *Marketletter*, February 27, 1995; "S'pore Must Tighten Patent Laws, says Glaxo," *Business Times*, December 1, 1994; due to international pressure, however, Singapore will align its patent and copyright regulation with the international agreement on Trade-Related Aspects of International Property Rights (TRIPS) before the year 2000 deadline ("Singapore Regulations: Stronger Patent, Copyright Protection Pledged," *Economist Intelligence Unit*, June 22, 1995).

15. See Greg Mastel, "The Art of the Steal," *Washington Post*, February 19, 1995, C03; and Thomas R. Howell, Jeffrey D. Neuchterlein, and Susan B. Hester, *Semiconductors in China: Defining American Interests* (Washington, DC: Semiconductor Industry Association and Dewey Ballantine, 1995), 61–70, 92–96.

16. Such practices are also arguably inconsistent with the investment provisions of the WTO. Quote from *U.S.-China Memorandum of Understanding*, Article II.

17. John Jackson, *The World Trading System: Law and Policy of International Economic Relations* (Cambridge, MA: MIT Press, 1994), 94–95.

18. "Kodak Urges Japan to Consult U.S. Government on Trade Case," *Business Wire*, December 21, 1995.

19. Stuart Auerbach, "Raising a Roar Over a Ruling; Trade Pact Imperils Environmental Laws," *Washington Post*, October 1, 1991, D01; Peter Behr, "Environmentalists Find NAFTA Is No Easy Call; National Groups Remain Sharply Divided," *Washington Post*, August 24, 1993, C01.

Part II

Antidumping Laws

Chapter Ten

U.S. Antidumping Laws

Since the late nineteenth century, the U.S. government has been concerned with ensuring fair and balanced competition in the marketplace. Several generations of antitrust legislation, including the Sherman Act, the Clayton Act, and the Robinson-Patman Act, were passed to ensure fair competition within the domestic marketplace. Concern did not end at the border. If the prospect of a U.S. company driving its domestic rivals out of the market raises concerns, the prospect of that same conduct by a foreign company—beyond the reach of U.S. laws—raises even greater concerns. Not surprisingly, in the same era in which the U.S. government passed major antitrust legislation, it also passed the Antidumping Act of 1916 to ensure that foreign intervention in the marketplace was policed.[1]

Antidumping laws are designed to combat unfairly traded imports by imposing offsetting duties on imported products that are sold at prices below those at which they are sold in their home market or below the cost of producing the product. Antidumping laws are part of a system of American trade laws, including Section 301 and countervailing duty laws, that promote the principles of fair competition and open markets.

Antidumping laws are subject, however, to more criticism than the other trade laws. Perhaps this is due to the fact that antidumping laws require the imposition of a duty, which creates the impression of a protectionist effect; perhaps it is due to the difficulty many have in understanding why products that are priced artificially low may be a threat to the U.S. economy; or perhaps it is due to the complex administrative procedures involved in the operation of antidumping laws, which can create the impression of arbitrariness and arouse suspicion on the part of U.S. trading partners. Most likely, it is a combination of all of these concerns that brings antidumping laws in for sharp criticism, particularly by academics.

The principle of combating predatory pricing and price discrimination aimed at dominating targeted markets, however, is a well-accepted objective of U.S. antitrust laws. At their core, antidumping laws merely extend this principle, which underlies American antitrust laws, to international commerce. To understand the link between antitrust and antidumping laws, it is important to appreciate that dumping is normally not an isolated act, but a tactic in a larger commercial strategy that has to be supported by trade barriers, subsidies, or collusion. The United States uses antidumping laws as one of its principle tools to ensure that its commitment to open markets and free trade is not exploited by cartels and predatory mercantilists. In the same vein, antidumping law—rather than being a means of protectionism—supports America's liberal trading system.

The Uruguay Round multilateral trade agreement and U.S. law define dumping in the United States, as the selling of imported products in the U.S. market for "less than fair value." Less than fair value is defined as: 1) selling in the U.S. market at less than the home market price, 2) in the absence of a home market, selling at less than a third market price, or 3) in the absence of a reliable basis for making comparisons with either of the above, less than the cost of production.[2] For products originating from nonmarket economies (NMEs), the market-based benchmarks of dumping are sometimes not appropriate since there is no market from which production costs can be determined. In these situations, the nondumped price is defined by the production costs in a comparable market economy.[3]

In cases where dumping is found and the dumped products are found to cause injury—normally after a petition from a competing U.S. industry is filed and an investigation is held—the U.S. government responds by imposing antidumping duties sufficient to bring the total price of the dumped goods up to the appropriate nondumped price

(price in the home market, price in third market, etc.). In instances where dumping is found, exporters may choose to enter into a "suspension agreement" with the U.S. Commerce Department—with the acquiescence of the petitioning domestic industry—to raise their price to a nondumping level, instead of facing the actual imposition of the duties.[4]

In order to comply with the provisions of GATT's, now WTO's, code on dumping, the United States imposes a two-step process for administering antidumping laws. Two agencies are involved. The U.S. Commerce Department, an administrative agency, determines if dumping is taking place, assigns offsetting duties—commonly known as dumping margins—and administers suspension agreements. An independent federal agency, the International Trade Commission (ITC), determines if dumped imports are a source of "injury" to competing domestic industries. The second function, applying an injury test, is a requirement of the WTO (and formerly part of the GATT Antidumping Code, though the United States actually adopted the practice before it was required) and has the effect of terminating many otherwise valid antidumping cases.[5]

The two agencies perform their functions in parallel. Both conduct their administrative procedures with opportunities for input from the petitioning company(s) and interests, the company accused of dumping (respondents), and allied interests. Once a dumping petition is filed, the ITC acts first to make a preliminary determination of injury. The test applied at this preliminary stage is fairly low, with the commission looking for reasonable indications that imports may be causing injury.

If the preliminary ITC determination is affirmative, then the case goes to the Commerce Department. The Commerce Department makes a preliminary determination of whether dumping is occurring and the size of the dumping margin. If dumping is found after further review, the Commerce Department issues its final determination on dumping and assigns a final dumping margin. At this point, duties can be assessed (though they are not final until the ITC's final determination). In lieu of duties, the U.S. Customs Service can require posting of a bond in anticipation of the ITC's ruling. (This is also the stage in the process where suspension agreements are sometimes struck.)

The ITC then issues its final decision on injury, at which point it may take into account not only present injury but also the imminent threat of future injury based on such factors as rapid growth in imports and the size of the Commerce Department's suggested margin. If the ITC's final determination is affirmative, the collected duties remain in the U.S. Treasury (or the bond is forfeited). If the ITC's final ruling is negative, the collected duties (or the bond) are returned.[6] The total length of the case from initial filing to a final ITC determination is usually less than 280 days, though in complex cases the deadlines can be longer and in "critical circumstances" can be accelerated. See Table 10.1.

Table 10.1 **Summary of U.S. Dumping Determination Procedures**

Petitions Filed/ Investigation Begins	Preliminary Injury Determination (ITC)	Preliminary LTFV Determination (DOC)	Final LTFV Determination (DOC)	Final Injury Determination (ITC)
DAY 1	**DAY 1–45** *(45 days)*	**DAY 45–160** *(115 days)*	**DAY 160–235** *(75 days)*	**DAY 235–280** *(45 days)*

- At each stage, a positive or negative determination is made. If negative, the case is dropped, except at the Preliminary LTFV (less than fair value) Determination. Here, if determination is negative, the investigation continues, allowing the DOC the opportunity to change its preliminary view in light of subsequent information.

- After the Final Injury Determination is made, duties are imposed.

Source: U.S. International Trade Commission, *Annual Report, 1993.*

Notes

1. The Antidumping Act of 1916, ch. 463, sec. 801, 39 Stat. 798, 15 U.S.C. 72.
2. U.S. antidumping law from: Subtitle B of Title VII of the Tariff Act of 1930, 19 U.S.C. 1673-1677, Pub. L. 71-361, as amended by Pub. L. 96-39 (Trade Agreements Act of 1979), Pub. L. 98-573 (Trade and Tariff Act of 1984), Pub. L. 99-514 (Tax Reform Act of 1985), Pub. L. 100-418 (Omnibus Trade and Competitiveness Act of 1988), Pub. L. 100-647 (Technical Corrections of 1988 and Miscellaneous Revenue Act of 1988), Pub. L. 103-465 (Uruguay Round Agreements Act of 1994). See Appendix E.
3. 19 U.S.C. 1677b(c).
4. 19 U.S.C. 1673c(b).

5. "Agreement on Implementation of Article VI of the General Agreement on Tariffs and Trade 1994," *Final Texts of the GATT Uruguay Round Agreements*, Article 3, 148–50.

6. 19 U.S.C. 1673b(d).

Chapter Eleven

Rationale for Antidumping Laws

Probably the most perplexing question for the casual observer is "Why do companies dump?" This question goes right to the heart of the controversy over antidumping laws, and the answer to the question directly influences one's view on the desirability of antidumping laws. On the one hand, opponents of antidumping laws will assert that all or most antidumping actions are simply the result of arbitrary U.S. laws, pernicious actions by government officials administering the laws, and harassment of legitimate commerce by protectionist-minded U.S. companies. On the other hand, proponents assert dumping is the result of predatory foreign firms' efforts to drive U.S. competitors out of business in order to gain control of the market and raise prices.

Both viewpoints overstate the case. Most dumping cases cannot be explained from either of these extreme perspectives. In fact, dumping is not the result of one phenomenon, but of several. In practice, companies engage in dumping for a range of reasons, and dumping can be part of several commercial strategies. It is normally the result of a larger market strategy aimed at disposing of surplus production, gaining a market foothold, responding to government direction, or depressing competitors' earnings. In order to give the reader a sense of the range of motivations and behaviors involved, and the continuing need for antidumping laws, this section breaks dumping motivations into four categories and draws upon real-world examples to illustrate them, then addresses some of the common criticisms of antidumping cases, such as complaints of administrative bias.

Of course, the real world does not always break into clear categories. Companies involved may arguably be dumping for two or more of the listed motivations. Nonetheless, the four categories this chapter describes will give readers a better understanding of the motivations behind dumping. The four categories are: 1) overcapacity dumping, 2) government-sponsored dumping, 3) tactical dumping and price discrimination, and 4) predatory dumping.

Overcapacity Dumping

Many critics of the antidumping law argue that dumping is normal business practice and should not be punished. Instead, the United States should simply enjoy the consumer benefits of low-priced goods. To the casual observer it may seem counterintuitive for a profit-driven company to sell at a loss, as is often the case when a company engages in dumping. In actuality, however, there is a rational economic basis to critics' claims on this issue.

As any beginning economics text will make clear, every manufacturing firm runs two kinds of costs: variable costs (costs directly linked to production, like raw material costs and manufacturing labor) and fixed costs (plant and equipment). In the short run, it might make sense for a business to continue to produce even when it was not covering its fully allocated costs (variable plus fixed), provided it was at least covering its variable costs. This makes economic sense for the company because fixed costs are generally sunk costs—meaning the costs have already been incurred and cannot be reduced even by halting all production. Ceasing production would thus not eliminate the fixed costs. In the short term, from the individual company's perspective, it would make sense to continue producing and selling even if the sales would not cover all costs but would cover variable costs and make some contribution—however small—to covering fixed costs. Under these circumstances, continuing production would leave the company in better shape because it would not have to take the entire fixed-cost expenditure as a loss, as it would have to do if it shut down completely. The company would still operate at a loss, but it would be a smaller loss than halting production.

This situation is not merely theoretical. It occasionally is faced by many manufacturing companies, and it is a problem often faced in declining industries where there is a built-in capacity to produce far more of a product than the market demands. Chronic excess capacity, for example, is one reason antidumping actions are so common in the steel market. Steel companies—particularly in Japan, Europe, and Korea—have built up large steel production capacities, often with government help, and often find themselves in a situation in which they are better off producing and selling even if the sale price does not cover the full cost of production.[1]

If these foreign steel companies are doing no more than following normal commercial practices in dumping steel—practices likely followed by U.S. steel companies too—why should antidumping duties be assessed? This is a valid question, but there are several valid answers.

First, merely because a practice might be rational for a business to undertake under some circumstances, in and of itself, does not mean a government—particularly if the company involved is in another country—should not act to counter the practice if it harms the larger national interest. Polluting and engaging in collusion can also increase profits but are often prohibited by governments because they are counter to the national interest. The same case can easily be made with regard to dumping.

Second, sales below cost should be only a short-term phenomenon in a free marketplace.[2] Companies cannot afford to continue operating at a loss indefinitely; unless prices improve, they must cut back capacity by closing factories and laying off workers. Government subsidies, trade barriers, and toleration of cartels, however, also play a role in delaying the adjustment, because this direct and indirect government assistance allows companies to put off adjustments dictated by the market and continue to operate at a loss. Since, in the case of the steel industry, the overcapacity problem has existed for more than twenty years, and since there is strong evidence that plants and sometimes whole national steel industries have continually operated at a loss through that period, there can be little doubt that government support has played a critical role in preserving steel overcapacity. One frequently cited estimate of total foreign government subsidies to the steel industry since 1980 is $86 billion.[3] In the case of the steel industry, then, antidumping cases are, in large part, a response to other governments' attempts to distort the marketplace, practices that are detrimental not only for U.S. steel producers but also for the efficient functioning of the free marketplace. Viewed from this perspective, antidumping margins are not protectionist tariffs, but counterbalances to market distortions.

Third, through continual dumping, foreign steel producers are choosing to put off adjustment. Ultimately, unless government intervention is permanent, the market will not be denied: less efficient plants will close, market prices will return to levels at which efficient producers can operate, and dumping complaints will decrease. In fact, this adjustment has already largely occurred, at least in the U.S. steel market.[4] Despite temporary import restraints in place from 1984 to 1992, the U.S. steel market has historically been relatively open to imports. Other countries insulated their steel producers from adjustment through subsidies and protection. By depressing steel prices within the U.S. market, foreign producers effectively shifted a disproportionate share of the ultimate cost of adjustment—unemployment—to be borne by the U.S. steel industry and the U.S. government—through unemployment compensation costs. Without the operation of antidumping laws, the U.S. steel marketplace would likely become a true dumping ground for foreign steel. The cost of adjustment in the United States is debatable, but there can be little debate that without the operation of antidumping laws, adjustment costs in the United States would have been significantly higher.[5]

The steel example is probably overused in the debate on antidumping laws. It does, however, clearly illustrate that although dumping may be a rational response by a *company* to an overcapacity situation, it does not follow that allowing dumping is the correct response for the *U.S. government*. Especially in light of market distorting actions taken by other governments that often delay the adjustment dictated by the marketplace, dumping laws can actually *restore* the operation of the free market, not *undermine* it.

Government-Supported Dumping

Dumping is a close relative of government subsidies, and countervailing duty (antisubsidy) laws closely parallel antidumping laws. A surprising number of products are routinely sold below the market-based cost of production because of heavy government subsidies. As just noted, subsidies are an important reason dumping has been such a common practice in the steel market—particularly in European companies. The European Union, the United States, Canada, and most other agricultural exporting countries routinely sell agricultural products well below the cost of production as a result of government subsidies.[6] Europe's commercial aerospace manufacturer, Airbus Industrie, in more than two decades of operation has repaid little of the government's investment on any of the eight generations of jet aircraft it has manufactured. Airbus's artificially low sales prices are also supported by government subsidies.[7] Unfortunately, this is hardly an exhaustive list. These examples should make it clear why antidumping and countervailing duty actions are frequently pursued in tandem: they are attacking the same market distortion.

The distinction between dumping and subsidies becomes particularly blurred when dealing with state-run (communist) economies or NMEs. In China, for example, the government still sets prices and wages throughout much of the economy. The market value of simple inputs within China, like a kilowatt hour of electricity or an hour of skilled labor, is literally impossible to determine.[8] The U.S. Commerce Department has experimented by applying countervailing duty law to trade with China, and there is a special provision of U.S. trade law—Section 406—for addressing trade with NMEs. However, because of its long operating history, reliable deadlines, and certainty of action once dumping is identified, antidumping law has been the primary tool for policing trade with NMEs. As a result, the Commerce Department has developed procedures for evaluating dumping by NMEs, including the practice of determining if dumping is occurring by comparison with "surrogate" market-economy producers.[9]

Historically, trade with NMEs has been limited. But since the mid-1970s, China has been attempting to expand trade with the United States and other western countries. A large number of new dumping cases has been one result of the expansion. The causes behind Chinese and other NME dumping are twofold. First, the price of inputs—particularly labor and energy—has been unreasonably low when judged against external benchmarks. Second, as the World Bank pointed out, China's approach to trade policy so far has been "mercantilist," i.e., motivated by achieving export growth for the sake of generating foreign exchange without sufficient regard to costs.[10] Much of China's exports to the world are managed through state trading companies with a goal of acquiring hard currency—i.e., western currency. In their efforts to achieve this objective, state trading companies often have little regard for the true cost of the goods that are provided directly by the government.

For nearly a decade, China has been a major source of antidumping cases; it has consistently been among the top five targets of antidumping actions by U.S. petitioners. Moreover, in the last year, *more than a third of all cases filed have been directed against Chinese exports* (see Table 11.1). As one prominent trade lawyer who works primarily for respondents put it, "A strong case can be made that virtually every product exported by China is dumped."[11]

Table 11.1 **Comparison of Top Respondent Countries of Dumping Complaints (cases filed), 1984–93 and 1994–95**

Country	1984–93	1994–95
China	33	14
Japan	62	7
Korea	40	3
Taiwan	40	2
Brazil	37	7
Germany	29	2

Sources: U.S. International Trade Commission, *Annual Report 1993, 1994;* USITC, *Operation of the Trade Agreements Program,* 1985–93.

Although China is clearly the major focus of NME antidumping actions, others are emerging. The economies of Russia and the other former Soviet republics are making the transition toward market economies, but it is likely to be a long transition and they have quite a way to go. In the meantime, Russia—like China—has been attempting to build up hard currency reserves through trade. This effort has created a serious threat to the U.S. aluminum industry.[12] Aluminum production has long been a major Russian industry, and the major input into aluminum production is energy, which is supplied in Russia by state-built hydroelectric and nuclear plants, vestiges of the old Soviet system. To forestall antidumping cases in the United States and around the world, a worldwide aluminum market-sharing agreement was negotiated by Russia and other aluminum producers. A similar issue is now arising because a former manufacturer of Russian military aircraft is attempting a transition to production of large commercial aircraft in potential competition with U.S. aircraft producers.[13]

In light of the numerous remnants of state sponsorship in Russia, the other former Soviet republics, and throughout eastern Europe, and the desire of these same countries to generate sales and hard currency through exports, future antidumping and countervailing duty cases are a virtual certainty. Indeed, there is every reason to believe that the problem of NME dumping will grow in importance. By the turn of the century, the number of NME and transitional economy dumping cases could well eclipse more traditional dumping cases.[14]

Tactical Dumping and Discriminatory Pricing

Discriminatory pricing is the practice of selling the same product in different markets at different prices. As any beginning economics text will attest, discriminatory pricing is a profit-making strategy for monopolies and other firms under certain market conditions. The practice is restricted, however, within the U.S. market by the Robinson-Patman Act—an extension of U.S. antitrust law—on the basic theory that discriminatory pricing could be used by large companies to drive smaller competitors out of business and create a less competitive marketplace.[15]

The tactical use of discriminatory pricing is frequently described in business texts as a legitimate market strategy in certain instances. For example, in the 1970s two tire companies—Michelin, a European company, and Goodyear, a U.S. company—engaged in competition for the U.S. tire market. Michelin, on the strength of strong sales in Europe, attempted to make a major entry into the U.S. market by sharply cutting tire prices. Goodyear, instead of responding by matching Michelin's price in the United States, chose to lower prices in the European market. In Europe, Goodyear had a small market share and Michelin a large share, and thus Goodyear could lower the competitive market price on a comparatively small volume of sales, and force Michelin to match the price on its much larger volume of European sales. This tactical move—essentially countering dumping with dumping—worked well; Michelin's profits were driven down, and it was forced to slow its expansion into North America. For a variety of reasons, neither company ever chose to file dumping cases against the other.[16]

Not all companies, however, have the ability to beat back dumping on their own, either because of their size or because the home market of their competitors is relatively closed to imports by trade barriers. Discriminatory pricing works best if a company has a secure home market that is relatively closed to imports. With a closed home market, a company can charge relatively high prices at home and generate high profits, which, in turn, subsidize sales at a loss in export markets in order to gain market share. The term for this practice is cross-subsidization. An open home market would leave the company in this example vulnerable to counter-dumping (as was carried out by Goodyear in the example above) and even the re-exportation of dumped goods back to the home market. This explains why the country of origin for the companies most frequently cited under U.S. antidumping law are countries most frequently accused of protectionism at home—Japan, Korea, Brazil, Taiwan, and China.[17] Protectionism at home makes dumping a viable export strategy.

An excellent recent example of how protectionism can support dumping and how antidumping laws can correct the imbalance is found in the dumping dispute between Eastman Kodak and Fuji Film. Eastman Kodak—a U.S.-based company—is the dominant producer of film in most markets in the world, with the notable exception of Japan. In Japan, Fuji Film, a Japanese film company, dominates the market. In recent years, Fuji has moved to expand its market share around the world. As part of this strategy, it began dumping in the U.S. market. This dumping successfully forced Eastman Kodak to cut prices to defend its market share and, in turn, decreased profitability and limited the resources the company had to defend other markets around the globe. Eastman Kodak was blocked from responding in kind within the Japanese market by a wide variety of Japanese nontariff barriers to film imports, most notably a great difficulty in penetrating the Japanese distribution system.

Eastman Kodak filed a dumping case against Fuji, which was successfully settled in a suspension agreement in August of 1994.[18] The suspension agreement allowed Eastman Kodak's market share and profitability to recover in the U.S. market and put it on an even footing with its global competition. Eastman Kodak has increased efforts to sell in Japan through tactics such as manufacturing film for other store brands, as a way to gain increased market access and make it more difficult for Fuji to dump from a secure home market. Eastman Kodak has also stepped up efforts to confront Japanese trade barriers by filing an unfair trade complaint—a Section 301 petition—to enlist the U.S. government's assistance in opening the Japanese market.[19] The Kodak-Fuji competition is an excellent case study of antidumping laws being used to counter protectionism and dumping.[20]

In the cases of tactical price discrimination, antidumping laws serve two important functions. First, they are an international extension of the Robinson-Patman Act's objective of ensuring a diverse and competitive market that rebounds to the ultimate benefit of consumers and producers. Second, instead of being, as critics assert, a protectionist device, they are an effective tool for countering the adverse effects of protectionism abroad within the U.S. market. As long as markets remain closed to U.S. exports, antidumping laws will remain a critical protection to keep U.S. firms from falling victim to cross-subsidies made possible by foreign protectionism.

Predatory Dumping

Predatory dumping, as the term is used in this book, is an extreme form of discriminatory pricing. In fact, most of the preceding discussion of discriminatory pricing is fully applicable. The distinction made here, however, is that discriminatory pricing is a commercial tactic aimed at market entry or suppressing profitability in order to limit competitor operations using profits generated in a closed home market or with the help of government subsidies. Its likely objective is to gain market advantages but not actually to eliminate the competition entirely. Predatory pricing goes one step further and aims to eliminate the competition with the objective of gaining exclusive or near-exclusive control of the market, presumably to allow monopoly profits to be extracted in the future. This is what the layman probably thinks of as dumping, to the extent the layman thinks about dumping at all.

Although most foreign companies engaged in dumping would probably be quite happy to drive their competitors out of business and dominate the market, this is not usually their immediate objective, and the scale and duration of dumping is not sufficient to achieve that objective. There are, however, exceptions. Japanese dumping of semiconductors in the early to mid-1980s seems a legitimate example of predatory pricing aimed at driving the U.S. semiconductor industry out of business,[21] as do Japanese efforts to dominate the television industry.

The highlights of the semiconductor dumping experience are as follows. In the late 1970s, Japanese companies began to move heavily into the semiconductor market, which was at the time dominated by U.S. companies such as Motorola and Intel. In the early 1980s, Japanese companies began to secure a portion of the U.S. market and eventually to dominate the market for memory chips, known as DRAMs, by sharply cutting prices. The price for DRAMs plummeted, and Japanese companies were hit with a long series of successful antidumping cases, with margins often exceeding 100 percent. The semiconductor technology, however, moved so quickly that new generations of DRAMs emerged before new dumping orders could be put in place. All but one U.S. semiconductor company was eventually forced to abandon the DRAM market. Most companies attempted to switch to logic chips, known as EPROMs. Japanese companies also began dumping in the EPROM market, and the U.S. semiconductor industry came dangerously close to collapse.[22]

The U.S. government responded in the mid-1980s by initiating both antidumping actions and Section 301 actions aimed at opening the closed Japanese semiconductor market. An agreement was ultimately negotiated to end dumping and increase U.S. sales in Japan. By the early 1990s, the agreement appeared largely to have succeeded. Dumping has generally abated, and now U.S. semiconductor exports to Japan are up, and the U.S. semiconductor industry is by most measures again the world's leader. There can be little doubt that the U.S.-Japan Semiconductor Agreement, which included the equivalent of a large suspension agreement to stop Japanese dumping, played a major role in preventing the destruction of the U.S. semiconductor industry.[23]

A less happy ending to an instance of predatory dumping involves the U.S. television industry. In the late 1950s, Japanese television manufacturers formed a cartel to control production and prices within the already protected Japanese market. After gaining licenses to key U.S. television technology in the early 1960s, Japan launched a major assault on the U.S. television market through dumping, using both low sales prices and rebates to distributors for televisions sold. The Treasury Department, which administered the antidumping laws at that point, did not even act on a dumping complaint until 1971—nearly three years after the antidumping petition was filed—and was unable to document the secret rebating practices. Primarily as a result of this dumping, employment in the U.S. television industry dropped 50 percent between 1966 and 1970 and another 34 percent by 1975.[24] In 1968, there were twenty-eight U.S. television manufacturers. By late 1976, only six had survived.[25] Japanese electronics firms used this strong foothold in television and similar pricing tactics to dominate the rest of the consumer electronics market, including VCRs (invented in the United States but manufactured mainly in Japan) and stereos. Japanese dominance is now so strong in some segments of the consumer electronics industry that there have been allegations of collusion to raise prices in the U.S. market.[26]

Few would argue that the U.S. government should not counter such direct efforts to destroy a major U.S. industry. Clearly, action in these instances is a direct extension of U.S. antitrust laws, benefiting both American industry and, ultimately, American consumers. If anything, the experience with Japanese semiconductor and television dumping would indicate that U.S. antidumping laws act too slowly in response to aggressive, predatory dumping—particularly in a rapidly evolving, high-tech sector. Predatory dumping is not the norm in dumping cases, but it is an eventuality that U.S. trade law must be prepared to recognize and address.

Harassment and Biased Administration

Some foreign companies and respondents' counsel take the position that a significant portion of dumping cases represent harassment filings by American companies seeking undue protection. Those advancing this argument also generally view U.S. laws, and administering authorities, as heavily biased in favor of petitioners and against respondents.

It is entirely possible that cases are sometimes filed with the expectation of winning concessions, such as convincing foreign companies to raise the market price—either voluntarily or as the result of a voluntary export restraint agreement. Clearly, avoiding dumping margins and the associated administrative burdens was a central reason both the U.S. Commerce Department and foreign steel producers agreed to restrain steel imports.[27] It was also a motive behind the recent worldwide agreement to divide the aluminum market. Using the antidumping law to deter or prevent dumping without an actual finding of dumping is not, however, an undesirable or even unintended consequence of dumping laws. The fact that foreign companies do restrain exports and raise prices when faced with an antidumping case can be taken as strong evidence that the foreign company was, in fact, dumping.

To support their claim of antidumping harassment, critics frequently allege that the Commerce Department engages in everything from bias to slipshod enforcement to flawed calculations, including making artificial comparisons between different products (comparing the price for a more sophisticated version of a product with more features to a stripped-down version of the same) or inflating the costs of production by assuming unrealistic overhead costs. Critics also argue that dumping laws are fundamentally slanted in favor of petitioning industries.[28]

Since U.S. dumping laws are written by the U.S. Congress, it is natural to assume that the authors are probably closer to the U.S. industries than to foreign interests. Petitioners' interests are well represented before the Congress, but they do not win all legislative battles; respondent interests have won their share.[29] Importers, foreign interests—including foreign governments—and U.S. companies that import raw materials have become increasingly active in legislative debates on antidumping laws, however, and also have effective advocates in Congress. Further, the laws passed by Congress must also comply with the terms of international agreements. Thus, to the extent it exists, systematic bias that favors petitioning industries could only occur within the limits set by international agreements.

In regard to bias in Commerce Department administrative decisions, there is a long record upon which to base judgment. Over the lifetime of U.S. antidumping laws, there have been hundreds of completed cases and many more that were terminated at earlier stages. In many of those cases, the Commerce Department was called upon to make complex administrative judgments. Under these circumstances, it would be unusual indeed if occasional errors were not made.[30] It is well beyond the pale of credibility, however, to assert that these errors account for a large portion of dumping cases, especially since Commerce Department decisions are subject to review by both the U.S. Court of International Trade and international dispute settlement panels under both the new World Trade Organization (formerly the GATT) and the North American Free Trade Agreement (if the case involves a NAFTA member).[31]

There may be cases in which antidumping actions have been filed to harass imports. Dumping is an expensive case not only to prove but also to defend against. Given the administrative protections to avoid baseless cases, however—the injury test, international review, etc.—it is a seemingly very expensive and risky approach to meeting foreign competition. Unless there is a reasonable expectation of proving dumping, investment in marketing or cost-cutting would seem to be a more cost-effective approach to counter foreign competition in most instances. Further, Justice Department and FTC officials have frequently stated that collusion to exclude imports through spurious trade complaints could result in prosecution under U.S. law.[32] No such case has ever been prosecuted, but the threats appear to be taken seriously by petitioners and provide another reason to avoid harassment dumping complaints.

Unfortunately, this is a difficult issue to assess analytically because no one has been able clearly to identify harassment cases. Numerous commentators have asserted that some cases are examples of harassing legitimate imports, but these claims are ultimately nothing more than assertions, subject to significant debate. For example, many commentators have cited U.S. antidumping actions against Swedish steel makers—who are portrayed as defenders of free and fair trade—as evidence of harassment by U.S. dumping complaints.[33] However, European administrative authorities, with no connection to, or particular love for, U.S. antidumping law, have found that Swedish steel makers have engaged in extensive collusion and other coercive business practices.[34] Also, only one of the several dumping findings against Swedish steel makers was overturned by the GATT, and that decision was based on a technicality in the filing of the case (the panel ruled that there was not evidence that the case had the support of the majority of the domestic industry). The GATT panel did not overturn the core claim that Swedish steel makers had dumped steel in the U.S. market.[35] Further, even if a company did generally take a free and fair trade posture, it might sometimes engage in dumping to achieve business objectives—particularly in an industry plagued by overcapacity. In short, trade harassment is normally in the eye of the beholder. Much as is the case with administrative errors, there likely are instances where harassment has taken place, but no convincing demonstrations of continuing harassment without basis have been demonstrated.

Notes

1. Lawrence Chimerine, Alan Tonelson, Karl von Schriltz, and Gregory Stanko, *Can the Phoenix Survive? The Fall and Rise of the American Steel Industry* (Washington, DC: Economic Strategy Institute, 1994), 55–62.

2. As noted, not all dumping cases involve selling below cost, many involve price discrimination—selling at a lower price in the U.S. market than in the home market. The number of cases involving sales below cost appears to be increasing, however, as nonmarket economies become an increasingly important focus of antidumping actions. Further, in instances of overcapacity dumping—the topic of this section—selling below fully allocated cost is a frequent occurrence.

3. *Testimony Before the United States International Trade Commission, Prepared Brief on Behalf of the U.S. Steel Industry,* by Dewey Ballantine and Skadden, Arps, Slate, Meagher & Flom, September 13, 1994. Another estimate of subsidies to the EC steel industry, 1980–85, is $38 billion (Thomas R. Howell, William A. Noellert, Jesse G. Kreier, and Alan Wm. Wolff, *Steel and the State* [Boulder, CO: Westview Press, 1988], 69). Other estimates of foreign subsidies to the foreign steel market are higher than $100 billion.

4. As discussed in *Can the Phoenix Survive?* U.S. steel is now much more competitive. A good example are the minimills, whose share of U.S. steel production has gone from 10.5 percent in 1965 to 30.4 percent in 1986. The minimills have been better able to adopt new technologies and, because of their size and capacity, did not have the adjustment problems faced by the integrated producers.

5. It is fair to say steel prices in the United States were generally lower than the market price for steel in Europe and Japan throughout the adjustment period. Thus, U.S. consumers likely bore a smaller proportionate burden than consumers in Europe and Japan.

6. Robert L. Paarlberg, *Fixing Farm Trade: Policy Options for the United States* (Cambridge, MA: Ballinger Publishing, 1988), 4–6, 13–32.

7. Gellman Research Associates, Inc., *An Economic and Financial Review of Airbus Industrie* (Jenkintown, PA: USDOC, September 4, 1990), 2–13. For additional discussion on Airbus subsidies, see Laura D'Andrea Tyson, *Who's*

Bashing Whom? Trade Conflict in High-Technology Industries (Washington, DC: Institute for International Economics, 1992), 155–216.

8. U.S. Department of Commerce, *Study of China's New Market Orientation and U.S. Trade Laws* (Washington, DC: USDOC, August 1989), 141–53.

9. Ibid., 137–41; 19 U.S.C. 1677b(c).

10. The World Bank, *China: Foreign Trade Reform* (Washington, DC: World Bank, 1994), 1.

11. Conversations of the author.

12. Erle Norton and Martin Du Bois, "Foiled Competition: Don't Call It a Cartel, But World Aluminum Has Forged New Order," *Wall Street Journal,* June 9, 1994, 1.

13. Jeff Cole, "Boeing Contests Loan Request for Russian Jets—Plane Maker Sees Danger in Backing for Engines from Pratt and Whitney," *Wall Street Journal*, March 6, 1995, A2.

14. In the near future, the practice of dumping in order to gain valuable hard currency may not be limited to NMEs. As a result of the dramatic instability of the peso and the uncertainty now associated with its exchange rate, there is worry that Mexican industries may be tempted to dump in the U.S. market in order to obtain U.S. dollars. This is the case in recent allegations of dumping made by U.S. tomato growers against Mexican tomato imports (Scott Pendleton, "Florida Growers Say Time Is Ripe to Stem Mexican Tomato Flow," *Christian Science Monitor,* April 12, 1995, 3; and "Researcher Says Mexico Exceeded Tomato Quotas," *Journal of Commerce*, April 12, 1995), and a similar case has been filed on steel (Debra Beachy, "Local Firm Says Mexicans Dumped Steel; Executive Says Actions Have Decimated a Good Market for Texas Companies," *Houston Chronicle*, April 6, 1995, 1).

15. A discussion of the Robinson-Patman Act can be found in: Terry Calvani and Gilde Breidenbach, "An Introduction to the Robinson-Patman Act and Its Enforcement by the Government," *Antitrust Law Journal,* Fall 1990, 765–75.

16. Gary Hamel and C.K. Prahalad, "Do You Really Have a Global Strategy," *Harvard Business Review,* July-August 1985, 139.

17. See Table 12.1 for countries with the highest volume of Section 301 cases initiated since 1985.

18. Wendy Bounds, "Fuji Photo Film Signs Accord on U.S. Pricing, Japanese Firm Will Raise Charges on Color Paper; Kodak, Konica Benefit," *Wall Street Journal*, August 22, 1994, A4; "Fuji Statement on Signing Suspension Agreements with Department of Commerce," *Business Wire*, August 19, 1994.

19. See Petition of Eastman Kodak Company Before the Section 301 Committee, Office of the U.S. Trade Representative, Washington, D.C., May 18, 1995.

20. A much more detailed description of the Kodak-Fuji dispute is provided in vol. 3 of the Prehearing Brief in the matter of *Color Negative Photographic Paper from Japan and the Netherlands* before the United States International Trade Commission (Investigation # 731-TA-661,662), August 17, 1994.

21. See Clyde Prestowitz, *Trading Places: How We Allowed Japan to Take the Lead* (New York: Basic Books, 1988), 26–70.

22. Ibid.

23. The agreement was originally quite controversial with U.S. computer makers, which argued that the agreement, by raising semiconductor prices, raised their costs and made them less competitive with their Japanese counterparts. The controversy has faded over time, however. The computer makers, perhaps out of a legitimate recognition of their own need for a U.S. semiconductor industry and perhaps out of a political recognition that the semiconductor industry had significant political influence in the U.S. government (or some combination of both), eventually joined hands with the semiconductor industry and made joint recommendations, ultimately accepted for the most part, to continue the U.S.-Japan Semiconductor Agreement in a revised form.

24. Prestowitz, *Trading Places,* 201.

25. Pat Choate, *Agents of Influence: How Japan Manipulates America's Political and Economic System* (New York, NY: Simon and Schuster, 1990), 87.

26. Paul W. Valentine, "Panasonic To Repay $16 Million To Settle Lawsuit," *Washington Post,* January 19, 1989, F01.

27. Howell et al., *Steel and the State*, 246, 530–34.

28. Congressional Budget Office Memorandum, *A Review of U.S. Antidumping and Countervailing-Duty Law and Policy,* May 1994, 5.

29. Although petitioners' interests were portrayed as the winner in the legislative battles on the Uruguay Round implementing legislation, many of the petitioners' proposals, including duty-as-a-cost (see Appendix D) and a proposal to transfer revenue from duties to petitioners, were defeated in Congress.

30. Critics of the antidumping law have also asserted that the fact that the ITC makes negative determinations more frequently than the Commerce Department is evidence of bias on the part of the Commerce Department. Given that dumping complaints are expensive to bring, industries bringing complaints normally have a good idea of whether dumping is occurring based on their own information on foreign market prices and their own cost information before the case is ever brought to the Commerce Department. It is thus not surprising they bring only cases likely to be affirmed by the Commerce Department. In the case of the ITC, the injury ruling is based in large part on the overall economic condition of the industry **after** the case is filed. A variety of unpredictable and unrelated macroeconomic factors come into play in the ITC's injury determinations that cannot be easily predicted by the industry. Thus, the petitioning industry more frequently calculates incorrectly in making its injury claim than in making its dumping claim. Commerce Department officials also note that they frequently can discourage domestic companies from even filing weak dumping cases.

31. The Tariff Act of 1930, as amended, section 516A.

32. Charles F. Rule (assistant attorney general, Antitrust Division, U.S. Department of Justice), "Reconciling Antitrust and International Trade Policy—Ensuring U.S. Competitiveness in the 21st Century," speech to the New York State Bar Association, January 27, 1988; Terry Calvani and Randolph W. Tritell, "Invocation of United States Import Relief laws as an Antitrust Violation," Speech to the Fordham Corporate Law Institute, October 3, 1985.

33. Gunnar Fors, "Stainless Steel in Sweden: Antidumping Attacks Responsible International Citizenship," in J. Michael Finger, editor, *Antidumping: How It Works and Who Gets Hurt* (Ann Arbor, MI: University of Michigan Press, 1993), 153–59.

34. *EC Commission Decision of July 18, 1990*, Official Journal No. L 220/28 (August 15, 1990).

35. "Frozen Pipes," *The Economist*, April 6, 1991, 69.

Chapter Twelve

Conclusions

The most important lesson to be drawn from these case studies is that antidumping laws, rather than being instruments for protectionism, can be part of a strategy to develop an open and competitive global trading system. Antidumping laws can work with countervailing duty laws, Section 301, and antitrust laws to promote open markets, expand trade, and put an end to mercantilism and protectionism. Unless antidumping laws are a full-fledged part of this strategy, however, the U.S. marketplace will be vulnerable to foreign protectionism through cross-subsidized dumping and could be ravaged by the emergence of NMEs, such as China and Russia.

Five central observations make clear the role of antidumping laws in this strategy:

Dumping is directly linked to other protectionist practices. As a commercial strategy, dumping is not likely to succeed if it is pursued in isolation. There may be occasions when individual companies faced with an overcapacity problem may, in the short term, turn to dumping for the reasons cited in chapter 11. No rational company, however, would continue a policy of dumping beyond the short term, absent of other factors. In many cases, as previously explained, dumped sales actually cost the dumping company money. The long-term, rational response to a marketplace so depressed that prices do not cover costs is disinvestment, not continued dumping.

The only instances in which dumping can be pursued as a long-term strategy involve government support through one of the following channels: 1) government subsidies, 2) a protected home market, or 3) government toleration of cartels. In these three instances, operating profits can be generated either through direct government payments or through above-market prices extracted in protected home markets. As demonstrated by the case studies, dumping is a very costly proposition unless it is supported by a protected home market. Otherwise, dumped goods could be re-exported to the home market at the dumped price, depressing profit margins at home and thwarting the objectives of the dumper. An open home market also leaves a company engaged in dumping vulnerable to counter-dumping, as occurred in the Michelin-Goodyear situation. It is thus far more than a coincidence that the countries topping the list of U.S. antidumping actions—Japan, China, Taiwan, Korea, and Brazil—are also those most frequently cited as having closed markets under another U.S. trade law, Section 301.[1] See Table 12.1.

Table 12.1 **Top Respondent Countries to U.S. Section 301 Cases and Successful Final Determination of Dumping, 1985–94**

Top countries as respondents to dumping cases, 1985–94. (final affirmative determination)	
1) Japan	39
1) China	23
3, 4) Brazil, Korea	18
5) Taiwan	14
6) Germany	13
7) India	9

Top Section 301 case countries, 1985–94. (cases initiated)	
1) Japan	8
2) Korea	6
3) Canada	5
4, 5) Brazil, India	4
6, 7, 8) China, Taiwan, Thailand	3

Sources: Section 301 public case files of the USTR's office; U.S. International Trade Commission, *Annual Report 1993, 1994*; USITC, *Operation of the Trade Agreements Program, 1985–94*.

Table 12.1 continued

Note: The European Union is not included in the Section 301 table. As a group of countries, it would be the most frequently cited (nine cases initiated since 1985), but 301 cases are brought against the union and not the individual countries. Dumping cases are brought against individual countries, and those have been included in the dumping table.

Dumping cases have also been brought against trading partners that maintain more open economies—Canada and members of the European Union—but antidumping actions against companies from these markets have generally been less frequent, considering the volumes of trade involved, and have been focused in those sectors in which these countries maintain trade barriers, such as the European steel and agricultural sectors, which are highly subsidized and/or protected.

In short, dumping as a commercial strategy is almost always directly linked with other types of protection. Companies pursuing a long-term dumping strategy build up profits at home in order to support foreign dumping. These high home profits can be built only with the help of subsidies, protection, or cartels. In the case of Japan, for example, the protected home market is the base used to support dumping. The regional profit breakdown for the Japanese auto industry (see Figure 12.1) is reported to be typical of other Japanese manufacturing industries (although less complete accounting data has been compiled in other cases) and demonstrates how a closed home market can provide a basis for dumping.[2] Dumping is generally only one part of a protectionist or mercantilist trade strategy to build market share, and antidumping actions are correctly viewed as efforts to combat these strategies, not as simple protectionism.

U.S. industries turn to antidumping laws because they are a reliable response to mercantilism. Antidumping actions are often pursued to counter unfair trade strategies, even in those cases in which dumping is not the core problem, because antidumping laws provide some certainty of action. In several examples cited earlier, such as the semiconductor and the Kodak-Fuji cases, dumping was only part of the problem. The core of the problem in these cases was, in fact, market-access barriers in Japan.

Figure 12.1 Geographic Source of Profits for Japanese Automakers

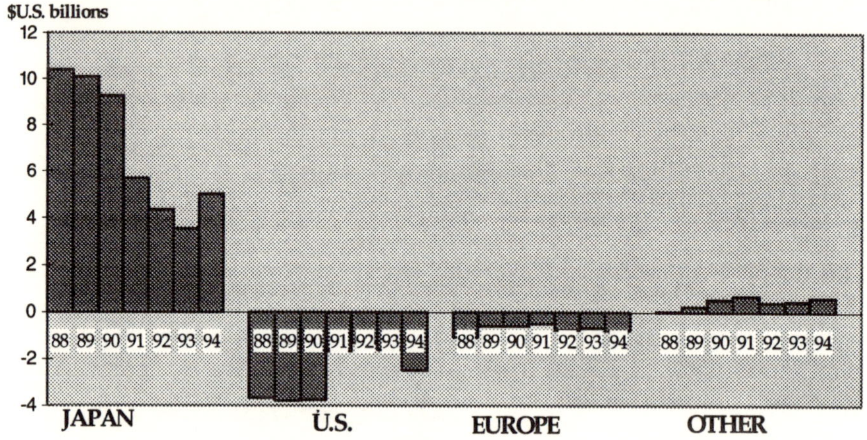

$U.S. billions, years 88–94 shown for JAPAN, U.S., EUROPE, OTHER.

Copyright © 1995 by Woodworth Holdings, Ltd. All rights reserved.
Woodworth Holdings, Ltd., Automotive Research.
1994 profit figures are preliminary estimates.
Reproduced with permission.

There is not, however, a reliable remedy for foreign market-access barriers. Section 301 of U.S. trade law is available to attack foreign trade barriers, but the Section 301 statute retains far more administrative discretion than antidumping laws, which require automatic action if injurious dumping is proven. Further, even if U.S. administrative authorities could be convinced to pursue a Section 301 case, there is no guarantee that the foreign government involved would dismantle its trade barriers. Countering dumping may often be an example of treating symptoms rather than curing the disease by eliminating the supporting trade barriers. Since there is no easy cure for the disease, however, U.S. companies often find it better to treat the symptom than simply to ignore the problem.

Antidumping actions are likely to increase in the future. Dumping will likely be a greater problem in the future as NMEs become an important force in the global economy. Over the years, the United States has made some progress in eliminating barriers to trade around the world. This, however, is no guarantee that dumping will cease to be a problem. In fact, there is good reason to fear that a number of current economic trends point to increased dumping cases.

Since an industry must prove economic injury in order to pursue a dumping case successfully, filings of dumping cases often tend to track overall business cycles—e.g., in periods of rapid expansion injury is hard to prove, and in economic downturns injury is easier to establish. Therefore, the number of cases filed in any particular year has as much to do with the business cycle as with changes in trading conditions.

The traditional motivations for dumping—overcapacity, discriminatory pricing, and predatory pricing—still exist, and since many markets remain relatively closed to imports, dumping is likely to continue to be a viable strategy for some foreign companies. The new addition to the mix, however, is increasing trade with NMEs. Trade with China appears likely to continue increasing at an almost exponential pace, and a number of other NME or transitional economies, like Russia, are poised to play an increasing role in world trade. Given that the degree of government involvement in these economies is likely to remain high and the price mechanism will continue to operate in only a limited fashion, increased dumping cases are the almost certain result. Antidumping laws are likely to be the only meaningful defense U.S. companies have from being injured by NME dumping.

In this light, the Clinton administration's proposal to exempt certain "transitional economies" from the antidumping laws seems particularly ill advised. The proposal—known as Economies in Transition (EIT)—would subject most transitional economies to another antidumping remedy, a remedy with an arguably higher injury standard and no guarantee of relief even if the standard is met.[3] The automaticity of the antidumping laws would also be replaced with wide administrative latitude. Interestingly, China was exempt from the proposal, perhaps because legislative strategists in the administration recognized that China was such a major target of antidumping actions that including it would render the proposal politically unviable. In short, this proposal would open a large hole in the antidumping laws, allowing EITs to dump just at the moment when EIT dumping is likely to become a major problem.[4]

This proposal is defended as an inducement to put EITs on the path to market reform by encouraging trade, but by removing the antidumping laws' built-in disincentive against government-dictated pricing, the proposal actually creates the reverse incentive, encouraging EITs to ignore market forces rather than to adopt a market-oriented system. The proposal might increase export revenues to EITs, but only at considerable cost to competing U.S. companies. The committees of jurisdiction in both houses of Congress rejected this proposal in August 1994, but there are reports that the Clinton administration plans to revive it.[5] With new commercial disputes having arisen with Russia, the EIT proposal seems very ill advised.

Antidumping laws' impact the economy. Some economists argue that dumping laws impose a high cost on the economy. The essence of their argument is the classic economic argument in favor of free trade: tariffs increase prices and thus reduce consumer welfare. The World Bank's chief economist, for example, compared the effect of dumping duties to the 1974 oil embargo. Both, he argued, increased the amount consumers paid for imports and thus reduced consumer welfare.[6]

This argument assumes an entirely one-dimensional view of the economy. If one assumes the policy of the U.S. government should always be to seek the lowest price, even if it is only a temporary price, then it does indeed make sense to scrap antidumping laws. It also makes sense to scrap environmental regulations, health and safety regulations, and most other government interventions in the economy. Laws against receipt and sale of stolen property would seem particularly vulnerable, because they have the effect of raising prices to consumers. Of course, critics will respond that laws against selling stolen property are necessary to combat the antisocial activity of stealing. This is, of course, absolutely true, but precisely the same argument can be made against dumping.

Under this logic, antitrust laws—a very close parallel to antidumping laws in this regard—should be eliminated to allow large companies to drive smaller competitors out of business and in the process lower prices for a time. Needless to say, this would be an extremely short-sighted strategy.

Similarly, eliminating antidumping laws would be extremely short sighted. The U.S. market would immediately become a more attractive dumping ground for industries experiencing an oversupply problem, which, in turn, would force the United States to bear the bulk of the adjustment costs in sectors such as steel and chemicals. U.S. industry would also be extremely vulnerable to mercantilistic commercial strategies pursued by companies from behind their home governments' trade barriers. This would likely make the U.S. market an unattractive place to produce semiconductors, computers, and film—to name only a few. Furthermore, these industries are unlikely to rebuild in the United States once dumping abates, even if they could pay the often high costs necessary to reenter a market (a very questionable assumption). Likewise, U.S.-based operations would permanently be vulnerable to dumping during a market downturn or another attempt by competitors to raise market share.

As is illustrated in Appendix B, many countries have adopted their own antidumping laws. The growing list of countries with antidumping laws was actually led by free-market-oriented economies, such as Canada, Australia, and the European Union. Two possible conclusions can be drawn from this. First, it could be concluded that all of the countries of the world are increasingly engaging in self-destructive policies to set back consumer welfare with no more thought for the eventual impact than lemmings give to following each other off a cliff. Alternatively, it also could be concluded that many countries—particularly those with otherwise open markets—see merit in insulating their marketplace and industries from the ravages of foreign protectionism and mercantilism.

Those economists who lump the antidumping laws with the oil embargo in terms of effect on the economy would apparently favor the first conclusion. This book takes the second view. Opening the marketplace to dumping would make the United States a hostile place indeed to establish a business operation, particularly in a world still populated by countries practicing protectionism and mercantilism and with the growing threat of serious market disruptions caused by the emergence of NMEs into the world economy. A simple numerical analysis of the impact of repealing antidumping laws is very difficult to make because it requires many complex assumptions about future economic and competitive trends. Just as the United States did when it adopted a vigorous antitrust policy, America and most other major trading economies have wisely decided that the temporary consumer costs to prevent dumping are a small price to pay to ensure a stable, competitive marketplace and a strong economy in the long term.

Short-term consumer costs must also be weighed against the significant cost of losing important manufacturing industries, which, under truly free trade, would continue to produce and to employ U.S. workers. For instance, what was the actual cost of losing most of the U.S. television industry and most of the production of VCR-related technologies? Precise figures are, of course, impossible to come by, but they could certainly run into hundreds of billions of dollars.

Certainly consumers and companies that rely on imported products as inputs have voiced loud complaints about antidumping laws. In fairness, it is possible to isolate a few cases where consumers or importing industries' interests were adversely affected by dumping decisions. As noted in an earlier section, there have been hundreds of dumping cases, and it is only to be expected that a few shortcomings in the law will come to light and a few administrative errors will be made.

These isolated examples, however, do not require a major overhaul of antidumping law. Barring an egregious error, the most consumers or purchasers of imported inputs are ever required to pay is the nondumped or fairly traded price. Since this is at least much closer to the price set by the market under normal conditions, it should be considered a normal market price and the dumped price considered an aberration. This is particularly true since the dumped price, for reasons already mentioned, is likely to be raised once commercial objectives have been achieved, probably to the long-term detriment of the consumer.

It is more than a coincidence that in one of the best-known examples of antidumping actions supposedly disadvantaging consumers—namely, the complaints of computer makers over the agreement to end semiconductor dumping—the users and the petitioning industries eventually reached an accord on the issue. This resolution could be a model for resolving similar disputes. In most cases, the consumers complaining are also the potential or actual customers of the petitioning industry. Thus, both sides have an incentive to settle the dispute amicably. Administrative authorities can seek to encourage these solutions by involving domestic petitioners and consumers, and through creative use of suspension agreements. A major rewrite of antidumping law to address this problem is unnecessary, however, and could well create more difficulties by increasing burdens on administrative decision makers and increasing litigation.

U.S. companies are victims of foreign antidumping actions. One of the prospects raised by opponents to strong antidumping laws is that U.S. companies could be hit by antidumping actions in foreign markets. There are certainly examples of U.S. companies facing antidumping actions in foreign markets, though it appears that the opponents of dumping laws are more concerned about the impact of antidumping laws on imports into the U.S. market than their impact on U.S. exports in foreign markets.

Still, as Appendix B makes clear, antidumping laws are increasingly being adopted around the world. An unfortunate reality of the modern world is that the U.S. tradition of open and transparent judicial and administrative processes is not widely shared. Even close U.S. allies, such as the EU and Mexico, have operated much of their dumping law as a "black box procedure"—i.e., the outcomes are announced, but the supporting procedures are not provided.[7] The European dumping law is written to provide significantly more administrative discretion and latitude in implementation than its American counterpart,[8] and there is reason to believe the Europeans have operated their dumping law to achieve trade policy goals other than merely stopping dumping, such as targeting an industry for protection or targeting a particular exporter.

As noted, U.S. exports have been subject to antidumping actions abroad. In some cases, the U.S. company involved might have been dumping for some of the reasons outlined above. In others, U.S. companies may be subject to arbitrary and capricious administration of antidumping laws. In the latter case, the United States has options. Foreign antidumping actions, like U.S. antidumping actions, can be reviewed under the WTO or—in those cases where they are available—by FTA dispute settlement bodies. Thus far, there is relatively little evidence of unfair foreign antidumping actions against U.S. firms—very few specific examples have been provided to support claims that this is a serious and growing problem.

If, however, this does emerge as a problem, the only appropriate remedy is seeking the appropriate international review of foreign dumping actions. Unilaterally weakening or eliminating U.S. antidumping laws is a very questionable route to the objective of securing fair and transparent operation of foreign antidumping laws. The United States was a leader in strengthening antidumping laws and developing the antidumping provisions of the WTO, but there is no reason to think other countries would follow the United States in retreat. The WTO endorses antidumping actions, and they are increasingly common around the world. To address legitimate concerns about the application of foreign antidumping laws, the United States should seek to press its trading partners to adopt open and transparent systems, like the United States, and not to scrap its own antidumping laws.

Notes

1. Super 301, a close relative of Section 301, is a U.S. trade statute that requires trade authorities to identify the most protected foreign markets. The United States took action against Brazil and Japan under Super 301, and action was threatened against Taiwan and Korea. China was not considered for action under Super 301 but is widely characterized as the most protected foreign market.

2. Auto imports control only about 4.6 percent of the Japanese auto market compared to 33 percent in the United States and 39–77 percent in other G-7 markets (*American Automobile Manufacturers Association*, 1994).

3. Peter Behr, "White House Seeks Change in Antidumping Penalties," *Washington Post*, June 25, 1994, B1; John Maggs, "White House Abruptly Seeks Major Dump Law Changes," *Journal of Commerce*, June 24, 1994, 1A.

4. Lynne M. Cohn, "Benedict Set to Tackle Dumping of Metal by Developing Nations," *American Metals Market*, August 24, 1994, 6.

5. Bill Schmitt, "Metals Industry Will Help Shape New Trade Law," *American Metals Market*, January 19, 1995, 12.

6. Hearing before the U.S. International Trade Commission by J. Michael Finger, Investigation no. 332-44 on the Economic Effects of Antidumping and Countervailing Duty Orders and Suspension Agreements, September 29, 1994.

7. Mark Joelson, "In the New Europe, A Shift in the Gears of Trade," *Legal Times*, June 20, 1994, 20; General Accounting Office, *International Trade: A Comparison of U.S. and Foreign Antidumping Practices*, November 1990, 25–34.

8. General Accounting Office, ibid., 20–22.

Chapter Thirteen

The Future of Antidumping Laws

Critics are anxious to discard antidumping laws on the scrapheap of history, arguing that such measures should be either abandoned entirely or replaced with the use of antitrust laws. In a perfect world free of trade barriers, government subsidies, and private-sector collusion, it would make sense to take a hard look at the continued necessity of antidumping laws.

The hard reality, however, is that the modern commercial world is a far cry from that perfect world. The U.S. Trade Representative's annual report listing foreign trade barriers is several hundred pages long and, by the admission of its authors, is far from exhaustive.[1] Government subsidies are not only prevalent but are actually defended as a critical tool of development and industrial policy by major trading partners, including Canada and the European Union. In fact, the WTO reflects that the current trend is toward tolerating certain subsidies as tools of national policy, not eliminating them.[2] The U.S. attitude on vigorous enforcement of antitrust laws is not shared by its major trading partners. The Europeans tolerate certain cartels as a matter of law,[3] and the Japanese have historically shown little interest in enforcing antitrust laws.[4] The increased role of formerly communist economies in the world economy is likely to increase the number of market distortions, particularly in the form of government subsidies.

As explained earlier, these trade barriers and subsidies are often the root cause of dumping.

The prospect of replacing antidumping laws with antitrust laws—in other words, treating foreign industries the same as domestic industries—would have appeal in the perfect world of economic textbooks, but it ignores two important realities. First, the real world is a far cry from the textbook models, and many of the economic assumptions supporting the textbook models are simply not shared by other major trading partners, which have their own, sometimes very different, textbooks. Foreign companies able to exploit home-market trade barriers and subsidies simply have more market power than a domestic firm. Domestically, all firms basically compete on a "level playing field," facing the same tax laws, government policies, etc. Internationally, the field is far from level.

Second, as stated at the outset, predatory pricing, discriminatory pricing, and other collusive behaviors should appropriately be subject to a higher degree of scrutiny when they involve efforts by foreign companies or foreign governments to control the U.S. market. In the domestic context, even if a firm could corner a market, it would not be beyond the reach of U.S. law; and if the government chose to break up a monopoly after the market had been dominated, it could be broken up by a court order. However, if a foreign company achieved market domination, the matter would in large part be beyond the reach of U.S. courts. A U.S. court succeeded in breaking up AT&T, but it would have much greater difficulty breaking up a trust built around Mitsubishi Heavy Industries (a Japanese company) or Airbus Industrie (a European company). Especially given the high entry costs and economy-of-scale advantages present in many industries, rebuilding a U.S. competitor to rekindle competition would be quite difficult indeed. Further, the concentration of important industries in foreign countries would raise national security concerns absent in the purely domestic context of antitrust law. Antidumping laws do uphold the same core principles of fair competition that underlie antitrust laws, but in the international context the lower standards and higher degree of scrutiny provided by antidumping laws are necessary and appropriate.

In short, the perfect world of free trade and fair competition is at best a dim mirage today. In the reality of a global marketplace riddled with market distortions, antidumping laws are a necessary and logical measure for a relatively open, subsidy-free, and trust-free market. Antidumping laws, by insulating U.S. industries from the negative impact of foreign protection, are a necessary safety measure to allow the U.S. economy to remain relatively open to trade. Rather than treating antidumping laws as the unwanted stepchild, advocates of free trade should embrace these laws as a necessary condition for the United States to continue its commitment to free trade.

Notes

1. U.S. Trade Representative, *1995 National Trade Estimate on Foreign Trade Barriers* (Washington, DC: USTR), 1–4.

2. John C. Danforth, "Trade Accord Should Be Renegotiated," *St. Louis Post-Dispatch*, February 13, 1994, 3B.

3. K.R. Mirow and H. Maurer, *Webs of Power: International Cartels and the World Economy* (Boston, MA: Houghton Mifflin, 1982), 150–58.

4. U.S. Trade Representative, *1993 National Trade Estimate on Foreign Trade Barriers* (Washington, DC: USTR), 144.

Part III

Countervailing Duty Laws

Chapter Fourteen

U.S. Countervailing Duty Laws*

Countervailing duty laws are often paired with antidumping laws by their critics. This pairing may seem logical at first glance, in that the laws are similar in form, impose offsetting duties, and are presently administered by U.S. Department of Commerce and the U.S. International Trade Commission. Beneath these superficial similarities, however, are fundamental differences between the two laws. Antidumping laws are targeted at countering predatory pricing of imports, while countervailing duties offset the effect of foreign government subsidies. Though a significant number of observers argue that dumping is not a problem warranting government concern, or even that it is beneficial for the United States, few are willing to make the same argument concerning government subsidies. When pressed on the matter directly, the same critics that lump antidumping and countervailing duty laws together will concede more sympathy for countervailing duty laws. Even some critics who advocate abolishing Section 301 and antidumping laws support the preservation of countervailing duty laws.

Perhaps critics are warmer to countervailing duty laws because they see foreign government subsidies as a more legitimate target of U.S. government action. Perhaps they recognize that, as a political reality, if the U.S. government does not respond to subsidies by imposing

---

*Rachel Hines contributed to this part

offsetting duties, it is likely to counter with domestic subsidies, which these critics find even more objectionable.

Whatever the motives, the United States has a long history of combating subsidies as a matter of U.S. trade policy. Current countervailing duty laws can trace their roots to measures the United States took in the 1890s to offset sugar subsidies.[1] Concerned references to foreign subsidies are found in U.S. congressional debates on international trade and trade treaties going back even further. The United States passed its first complete countervailing duty law in 1897,[2] and that law has since been revised frequently, with no less than ten important rewrites—normally focused on expanding coverage and improving operation—over the intervening years.

Since 1979 (arguably since 1930, although both have undergone substantial change since then), the operation of countervailing duty laws has closely paralleled the operation of antidumping laws. Under both, normally, cases are initiated by a private party that believes it is facing unfair import competition by a foreign government, but the U.S. government can self-initiate cases under unusual circumstances. Both are administered by two agencies, the U.S. Commerce Department's International Trade Administration and the U.S. International Trade Commission. The ITA determines whether or not the imported products in question are subsidized, while the ITC determines whether the product is imported in sufficient quantities to result in material injury to U.S. interests, poses an imminent threat of material injury to the industry, or materially retards the establishment of a domestic industry.[3]

Once a petition is filed, the ITA has a twenty-to-forty-day period to make a general, administrative assessment of the case. During this period, the domestic industry can be polled and the petition reviewed.[4] Once the petition is accepted, the ITC makes its preliminary decision on material injury first, and if that is affirmative, the ITA makes a preliminary decision on whether the product is subsidized. Whether or not a subsidy is preliminarily affirmed, the ITA goes on to make a final decision on whether or not a subsidy exists and its size. If the ITA decides a countervailable subsidy exists, the ITC makes its final decision. A bond posting is normally required after the ITA's preliminary decision, and a duty is imposed after the ITC's final decision. Again, as with antidumping cases, the ITA often enters into a suspension agreement with the exporter to discontinue or otherwise offset the subsidy instead of actually imposing a duty.[5] The entire process normally allows a total of 205 days from initiation of the case to the final ITC decision, but it can be longer in special cases. See Table 14.1.

Table 14.1 **Summary of U.S. Countervailing Duty Determination Procedures**

Petitions Filed/ Investigation Begins	Preliminary Injury Determination (ITC)	Preliminary Subsidy Determination (DOC)	Final Subsidy Determination (DOC)	Final Injury Determination (ITC)
DAY 1 The DOC has 20–40 days to accept petition.	**DAY 65** 25 days after the DOC accepts petition.	**DAY 65**	**DAY 160**	**DAY 205** The ITC has 120 days after preliminary DOC determination or 45 days after final DOC determination, whichever is longer.

-At each stage, a positive or negative determination is made. If negative, the case is dropped, except at the Preliminary Subsidy Determination. Here, if the determination is negative, the investigation continues.

-After a positive preliminary subsidy determination, a suspension agreement can be entered.

Source: U.S. International Trade Commission, *Annual Report, 1993.*

This description is intended only as an initial outline of the operation of countervailing duty (CVD) laws to allow readers to understand the following case studies and analysis. A more detailed analysis of the operation of CVD law, and other U.S. laws aimed at combating subsidies, is included in chapter 15 of this book.

Notes

1. 26 Stat. 567, Schedule E.237, 1890's law to offset sugar subsidies.
2. U.S. Tariff Act of 1897, 30 Stat. 151, Sec. 5.
3. The term *material injury* is used in the General Agreement on Tariffs and Trade and in U.S. law to establish the injury test. The precise meaning of the term

is clearly different to different ITC commissioners but generally should be taken to mean not-inconsequential injury. It is better understood in connection with a second, higher injury test—*serious injury*—that must be met before a GATT member country can impose temporary limits on fairly traded goods to allow adjustment of a competing domestic industry. In other words, to impose limits on fairly traded goods, a higher injury standard must be satisfied. The statute defines material injury as "harm which is not inconsequential, immaterial, or unimportant" [19 U.S.C. 1977(7)(A)].

4. This is a change that was made during the implementation of the Uruguay Round Agreement.

5. 19 U.S.C. 1671c.

Chapter Fifteen

Subsidies

Any discussion of the merits of countervailing duty law should appropriately begin with a discussion of subsidies. Countervailing laws exist only as a response to subsidies, and the purpose and function of the laws can only be understood in that context. Subsidies have been a concern of policy makers since the seventeenth and eighteenth centuries. Economists and political leaders have historically commented on the problems caused by subsidies—primarily of agricultural production—and included commitments against subsidies in treaties. The first, full countervailing duty law was passed by Belgium in 1892,[1] and a number of countries, including the United States, followed suit in the following decades.

Given the long history of discussions on the topic, one might expect that a fairly precise definition of the term *subsidy*—at least as the term applies to trade policy—would have been devised. Unfortunately, such is not the case. In fact, there is so much debate over the appropriate definition of the term that the GATT—the chief international agreement on international trade—was unable to settle upon a definition of subsidy until its latest round of negotiations in 1994. Even then, the definition was some 175 words in length,[2] and it is almost certain to be interpreted and elaborated upon by decision-making panels in the coming years. Previous to 1994, the GATT merely relied upon illustrative lists of various practices that would be deemed subsidies. U.S. countervailing duty laws historically took the opposite approach, defining a subsidy as a *bounty or grant* and allowing the Commerce Department to make the definition operational through administrative practice.

Most dictionaries settle upon a fairly narrow definition of *subsidy*, focusing on financial transfers between the government and private business. For example, the *Random House College Dictionary* (unabridged, 1980) defines it as "a direct pecuniary aid furnished by a government to a private commercial enterprise." This type of definition probably captures the word as it is normally used, but there are a number of cases in which government contribution is less direct. For example, the Canadian government has been found to subsidize its lumber industry by charging less than the full market value to cut timber from government land; there have also been a number of instances of government-directed subsidies being extended as loans offered to industry by private banks at below-market interest rates.

The definition of a direct financial contribution is thus too narrow to be useful in the context of defining what would be a countervailable subsidy. Conversely, a definition encompassing virtually anything that confers a benefit on the private sector may be too broad. For example, would a government's provision of highways and roads, or an educational system, constitute a countervailable subsidy? Both surely confer a benefit to the private sector, but, if taken as subsidies subject to countervailing duties, virtually all government activities, including the provision of national defense and police services, could be subject to countervailing duties. The test that has been devised to separate economy-wide subsidies from subsidies that may be countervailed is known as *general availability*.[3]

In short, general availability holds that only subsidies that have a narrowly targeted effect may be countervailed. This standard is not unambiguous. Countries subject to countervailing duties may argue that a subsidy that applies, in reality, only to specific industries is, in theory, generally available. For example, Canada argued that its timber subsidies were generally available because any industry could theoretically take advantage of the subsidy. Obviously, however, a right to cut timber at below-market rates is directly beneficial to the lumber industry and not beneficial to the computer industry or the aerospace industry. There are even more ambiguous cases. Subsidies

Subsidies   115

for university research in high technology may on occasion be ruled as generally available and in other cases be ruled a subsidy, depending on the nature of the subsidy and the nature of the research.

Wrestling with definitions of what is a countervailable subsidy and what is not has absorbed untold hours of trade negotiators' time. In 1979, the world trading system devised what is referred to as the Subsidies Code to cover subsidies and countervailing duties. The code was a voluntary side agreement to the GATT that expanded and clarified concepts relating to subsidies and countervailing duties that had been in the GATT text from previous negotiations and had arisen in conflicts subject to GATT dispute settlement. The code developed many new guidelines for subsidies and countervailing duties, but, most important in this context, it elucidated a better working definition of the term *subsidy*. The code also created what was known as the traffic light definition, delineating three categories of subsidies: red = impermissible; yellow = permissible but subject to countervail; and, green = permissible and not countervailable. The red, yellow, green formulation was not included in the code but was widely used by the negotiators and by subsequent commentators.[4]

The red, or impermissible, subsidies were primarily export subsidies or subsidies paid to encourage the export of a product. Most export subsidies were prohibited and were subject to GATT dispute settlement like all other trade barriers, although discipline on export subsidies of agricultural and other basic products was considerably more lax. Countries also had the option of countervailing red subsidies if the imports were causing injury to domestic industries. (The injury test was another important innovation in the subsidy code that is discussed at some length in chapter 20.) Yellow subsidies are often called domestic subsidies. These include subsidies normally tied to production and not to export, although the distinction can be blurry, since a strong domestic industry will normally export. These subsidies were not prohibited but could still be countervailed. Though U.S. countervailing duty law allowed broad coverage, the administrators at the ITA originally focused largely on direct export subsidies. As many direct export subsidies have been phased out and replaced with domestic subsidies, the domestic subsidies themselves have become the central focus of U.S. countervailing duty law.

The final category of green, or permissible, subsidies initially applied to subsidies that were truly generally available, such as national defense or a national highway system. (Although, as later discussion will make clear, the category has subsequently been expanded.) The permissible category was created in recognition that some subsidies served legitimate government purposes without creating substantial trade effects. The code also included illustrative lists to help define more clearly what negotiators had in mind for each category.[5] This basic three-category formulation has been preserved in subsequent negotiations and still forms the basis of the global trading agreement on subsidies.

Despite all the work that has taken place over the years to define countervailable subsidies, the definition continues to evolve. The new GATT definition of subsidies requires little change in U.S. practice, but some argue that one change is possible. The ITA has found in two different cases—one involving lumber from Canada and the other involving leather from Argentina—that a ban on the exportation of raw material (logs and cowhide in the cases mentioned) can confer a subsidy by depressing the domestic price of raw materials.[6] Some have interpreted the new subsidy definition as precluding this interpretation. There are counter-arguments that these export bans may be an instance in which the "government provides goods or services..." The issue is likely to be settled ultimately in litigation and/or dispute settlement panels. If the decision is to exclude these practices from the definition of subsidy, it will be unfortunate, since export bans on raw material, unless aimed at the preservation of natural resources or another legitimate purpose, seem clearly to be an example of a governmental practice conferring a specific, potentially trade-distorting benefit.

The ITA itself changed its definition of subsidy recently when it found that privatization of a formerly government-owned business could essentially eliminate the subsidy. The argument asserts that if the firm were sold at a market price, the price should reflect the fair value of all the firm's assets, including those provided through government subsidies. This analysis has some superficial appeal but seems to overlook the possibility that the full value of subsidies may not appear in its purchase price because of a variety of factors, including the government's decision on sales price. Furthermore, in valuing the future market potential of a firm (which results from many factors, including market prices of inputs and outputs that move in response to a wide range of economic forces, including potentially the presence of other subsidies in the market), the market may not fully reflect the value of government purchases of equipment, etc. A recent U.S. court decision has affected the ITA's privatization finding.[7] This issue is in no way related to the new subsidies definition. In fact, some language in the Subsidies Code would argue against the ITC finding. This example does indicate, however, that some marginal changes in the definition of countervailable subsidy are likely to continue in the future as new issues are confronted.

Notes

1. Jacob Viner, *Dumping: A Problem in International Trade* (Chicago: University of Chicago Press, 1923), 169.

2. From the *Final Texts of the GATT Uruguay Round Agreements,* "Agreement on Subsidies and Countervailing Measures," Part I: General Provisions, Article I: Definition of a Subsidy: "1.1 For the purpose of this Agreement, a subsidy shall be deemed to exist if: (a)(1) there is a financial contribution by a government or any public body within the territory of a Member (referred to in this agreement as 'government'), i.e. where: (i) a government practice involves direct transfer of funds (e.g. grants, loans, and equity infusion), potential direct transfers of funds or liabilities (e.g. loan guarantees); (ii) government revenue that is otherwise due is foregone or not collected (e.g. fiscal incentives such as tax credits); (iii) a government provides goods and services other than general infrastructure, or purchases goods; (iv) a government makes payments to a funding mechanism, or entrusts or directs a private body to carry out one or more of the type of functions illustrated in (i) to (iii) above which would normally be vested in the government and the practice, in no real sense, differs from practices normally followed by governments; or (a)(2) there is any form of income or price support in the sense of Article XVI of GATT 1994; and (b) a benefit is thereby conferred."

3. Gary Hufbauer and Shelton Erb, *Subsidies in International Trade* (Washington, DC: Institute for International Economics, 1984), 92.

4. Ibid., 22–24.

5. *Annex to the Code on Subsidies and Countervailing Measures,* Illustrative List of Export Subsidies.

6. See the *Joint Report of the Committee on Finance, Committee on Agriculture, Nutrition, and Forestry, and the Committee on Government Affairs of the United States Senate to Accompany S. 2467,* 103rd Congress, 2nd Session, 103 Senate Report 412, September 12, 1994, 90–91.

7. John A. Ragosta, Brent Bartlett, Michael R. Geroe, and John R. Magnus, *CVD Law From the General to the Specific: Some of the Significant Issues and Developments* (Washington, DC: Georgetown University, June 8, 1994), 20.

Chapter Sixteen

Subsidies around the World

The United States has been an advocate for subsidy discipline and countervailing duties since the beginning of the GATT negotiations. The primary reason for this is that the United States generally provides a lower level of subsidies—by any definition—than most other trading countries. This is not to say that the United States does not extend subsidies. As U.S. trading partners are quick to point out, the United States has provided significant agricultural subsidies for decades and provides smaller subsidies to develop certain technologies. Some of the United States programs were originally introduced to counter foreign subsidies; others had specific policy goals. Individual states and localities have also provided companies with various grants and tax benefits to convince them to settle in these states and localities. These subsidies occasionally gain some press attention, largely due to the promotion efforts of the politicians involved, but in economic terms, they tend to be relatively small. The Organization for Economic Cooperation and Development (OECD), an international organization composed of twenty-five member countries around the world, has tracked relative subsidies in major developed countries for decades and has consistently ranked the United States at the bottom of the list of subsidizers.[1] See Figure 16.1.

Figure 16.1 **G-7 Countries' Total Subsidies as a Percentage of Gross Domestic Product, Including Agriculture**

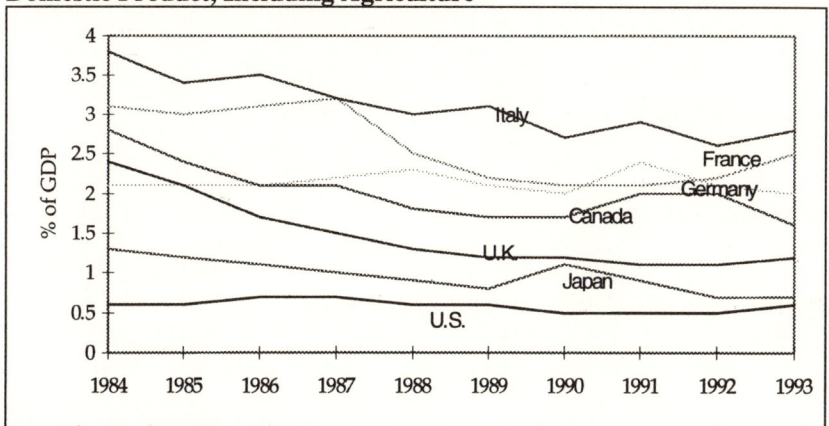

Source: OECD National Accounts, 1994.

In specific categories of potentially trade-distorting subsidies, such as export credits and trade promotion outside of the agricultural sector, U.S. subsidies are also quite small compared to other major trading countries.[2]

As is demonstrated in Tables 16.1 and 16.2, the actual level of subsidies in the United States fluctuates over time as the U.S. budgetary situation, U.S. policy toward subsidies, and foreign subsidy levels (perceived and real) change. In light of the current pressure to decrease government spending in the United States in order to decrease the U.S. budget deficit, U.S. subsidy levels seem likely to decline.[3] Agricultural subsidies have declined since the mid-1980s and are likely targets for further decreases. The Congress has recently eliminated several technology subsidies and is debating cuts in export credits and export promotion. U.S. subsidy levels as a percentage of GDP seem likely to be headed for a modern-era low in the next few years.

Table 16.1 **Official Export Credit as a Percentage of National Exports in G-7 Countries**

	1990	1991	1992	1993	Average
Japan	38%	35%	44%	37%	39%
France	20%	18%	17%	20%	19%
United Kingdom	18%	18%	3%	5%	11%
Italy	8%	10%	10%	3%	8%
Germany	4%	6%	6%	6%	6%
Canada	4%	3%	4%	4%	4%
United States	3%	3%	3%	3%	3%

Source: National Export Strategy, Report to the U.S. Congress by the Trade Promotion Coordinating Committee (DOC: October 1994); and calculations taken from a study by the Economic Strategy Institute, *U.S. Export Programs: Business Necessity or Corporate Welfare?, 1995.*

Table 16.2 **Nonagricultural Export Assistance Services of G-7 Countries, 1992**

	1992 Budget ($million)	1992 Exports ($billion)	GDP ($billion)	Assistance as % of GDP
United Kingdom	285.7	190.0	1008.0	0.028%
France	239.0	235.9	1322.0	0.018%
Canada	61.2	134.4	594.0	0.010%
Italy	71.2	178.2	1222.0	0.006%
Germany	83.9	422.3	1928.0	0.004%
Japan	94.3	339.9	3672.0	0.003%
United States	149.4	448.2	5951.0	0.003%

Source: National Export Strategy, Report to the U.S. Congress by the Trade Promotion Coordinating Committee (DOC: October 1994); and calculations taken from a study by the Economic Strategy Institute, *U.S. Export Programs: Business Necessity or Corporate Welfare?, 1995.*

Notes

1. OECD definition of a subsidy: All grants on current account made by government to private industries and public corporations; and grants made by the public authorities to government enterprises in compensation for operating losses when these losses are clearly the consequence of the policy of the government to maintain prices at a level below costs of production.

2. U.S. agricultural subsidies are more significant, although still lower than those of Europe and Japan, and have been declining sharply in recent years.

3. See Greg Mastel and Andrew Szamosszegi, *U.S. Export Programs: Business Necessity or Corporate Welfare?* (Washington, DC: ESI, 1995).

Chapter Seventeen

Subsidies As Trade Barriers

Because of the low level of U.S. subsidies, it has been sensible for the United States consistently to seek cuts in subsidies through international trade agreements and support strong countervailing duty laws in the United States. With the exception of efforts by the Clinton administration to allow certain subsidy programs to be exempt from countervailing duty law and "green lighted" in the Uruguay Round of GATT negotiations,[1] the United States has consistently advocated limits on subsidies in previous GATT negotiations (including those leading to the creation of the aforementioned Subsidies Code) and in bilateral negotiations, and was an early adopter of countervailing duty laws.

To the casual observer, this focus on decreasing subsidies in international trade negotiations may initially seem somewhat surprising. International trade negotiations are traditionally seen as forums for discussing the elimination of tariffs, quotas, and other measures that block imports. This view is certainly correct, but subsidies can distort trade as much or more than do these traditional trade barriers. The economic effect of subsidies is somewhat different from that of tariffs and quotas. Tariffs, for example, transfer wealth from consumers (who pay higher prices) and foreign producers (who lose sales because the tariffs force them to charge higher prices) to domestic producers (who benefit from higher market prices and decreased competition) and the government (which collects tariff revenue). In most cases, economists agree that the static losses to consumers and foreign producers exceed the static gains of domestic producers and the government.

Subsidies have a different economic effect. Subsidies for domestic production or exports transfer wealth from government treasuries and the taxpayers that support them (the source of the subsidy) and from foreign producers (who lose sales due to subsidized competition) to domestic producers (who increase production and/or sales) and to consumers, foreign and domestic (who pay lower prices). Again, though, economists agree that any distortion of the market generally results in a net loss of welfare—i.e., losses to the government and foreign producers exceed the gains to domestic producers and consumers. The market distortions caused by subsidies generally tend to result in misallocation of resources within the economy as well as too much of the subsidized good or service, and too little of nonsubsidized goods and services, in the country. (Conversely, in nonsubsidizing economies, too little is produced in comparison to market conditions.) Thus, heavy subsidies paid by a number of countries are probably the central reasons for continual problems of oversupply in certain sectors, namely agricultural products and steel.[2]

Some economists with a laissez-faire view of trade argue—as they do with regard to dumping—that countering and combating subsidies should not be a focus of U.S. trade policy. In their estimation, if other countries are willing to expend resources foolishly to provide U.S. customers with lower priced goods and services, the United States should just enjoy the consumer benefit. This view, while superficially appealing and still widely held in some circles, ignores three competitive, and political, realities in the current global trade environment.

First, subsidies act to distort trade and can be effective in buying a competitive edge, perhaps a long-term competitive edge, for domestic industries. Subsidies can induce industries to develop new technologies, build capacity beyond what is warranted by the market, and enter markets more quickly and on a broader scale. Critics of action to attack subsidies respond that the advantages gained from subsidization are likely to be erased by the market and replaced by underlying comparative advantage once taxpayers tire of shouldering the burden of subsidies.

Of course, the assumption that taxpayers will tire is not borne out by experience: agricultural subsidies have continued for decades. But even beyond that, this argument ignores the potential for subsidies to distort comparative advantage permanently. Subsidies can allow firms to exploit the so-called *first-mover* advantages of being a pioneer in new technologies or products, and exploit economy-of-scale advantages, by producing on a larger scale. If subsidies allow the firm to develop production technologies and drive competitors out of business, the barriers to market entry or re-entry may be too high for nonsubsidized competition. Thus, a subsidy can in some instances establish a competitive advantage that will be difficult or even impossible for nonsubsidized competition to match, even if the subsidies are later discontinued.

As the case studies in the next section demonstrate, subsidies have been successful in establishing competitive advantage in a number of instances. Europe has been able, with subsidies, to establish Airbus Industrie as a strong competitor in the worldwide, civilian aerospace industry. Europe was also successful in transforming itself from the world's largest net importer of agricultural products to the world's largest net exporter of agricultural products in less than a decade, through use of heavy subsidies. Japan has also relied, in part, on subsidies to target key sectors of its economy for development, often with good results. These subsidies, however, have often had serious, deleterious effects on their U.S. competitors, other nonsubsidized competitors, and the industries themselves. U.S. job losses in the civilian aerospace industry, steel, and a number of high-tech, otherwise competitive, industries can be traced, in large part, to foreign subsidies. Often, the effects have been very widespread. Global agricultural markets, for example, have been depressed by subsidies to the point where nonsubsidized competitors in developing countries have been driven out of business.

The diehard laissez-faire economist might still argue that, even if subsidies allow permanent domination within targeted industries, nonsubsidizing economies could simply move into other sectors. This argument gets to the heart of what has become known as the potato chips/computer chips argument—that it does not matter whether an economy is producing potato chips or computer chips, since both provide employment. The debate on this issue is fairly lengthy, and readers should explore another source for further information.[3] Suffice it to say, relatively few would defend this position as an absolute proposition. The evidence is strong that higher technology industries, such as semiconductors, not only create higher-paying jobs directly, but also lead to competitive edges in other, related high-tech and high-wage industries. Empirically, the fact that so many economies have been willing continually to spend money on subsidies in order to establish competitive advantages in the production of civilian aircraft, computer chips, and materials technologies—to name only a few—is strong evidence of a consensus that there are major economic benefits to establishing footholds in key industrial sectors.

A second reason that subsidies cannot be ignored by U.S. trade policy is that subsidies are increasingly being used to replace other, more traditional, trade barriers. Europe, for example, has, on a number of occasions, dismantled tariffs or quotas on particular agricultural products but then begun to pay heavy subsidies for production of the same products, thus having the effect of continuing the trade-distortion of the original trade barrier. The GATT has recognized the possibility of such chicanery for many years and has established a doctrine to address the problem. Article 23 of the GATT/WTO—commonly referred to as "nullification and impairment"—specifically addresses the problem of countries essentially dealing in what would be known as bad faith, in contract terms. Over the years, GATT dispute settlement panels have interpreted the application of subsidies to offset the effect of a trade concession—even if the subsidies were otherwise legal—to be a violation of the GATT. As other trade barriers are eliminated, the temptation to turn increasingly to subsidies for production is large, unless discipline on subsidies is also established.

Finally, few can dispute the political reality that subsidies tend to spawn counter subsidies in response. Often, countries find themselves in a cycle of increasing subsidies in order to counter the subsidies (perceived and real) of trading partners. It seems a near universal, political constant that countries are unwilling to allow themselves to be subsidized out of key industries. Whether or not one agrees with the decision to combat subsidies, it is impossible to dispute the fact that subsidies are often answered with subsidies, thus reducing welfare in all countries involved. To avoid these escalating cycles, subsidy discipline is essential.

Even in light of these three arguments, some would argue against countering subsidies with offsetting duties. The essence of this position is that two wrongs do not make a right or that two trade barriers do not make for a free market. This position, however, ignores the widely accepted economic concept of *second-best analysis,* a concept that holds that if an economic distortion cannot be eliminated, an offsetting distortion is often the best response. By way of classic example, if excessive pollution is produced by a particular industry because the cost of that pollution is not borne by the industry, the market failing can be corrected by imposing a tax on the industry to simulate the cost of pollution. Similarly, if a duty is imposed on subsidized imports, at minimum the negative effects of the subsidy can be kept out of the domestic market and unsubsidized domestic production be given a chance to compete fairly, at least at home. To address this market failing in other markets, a counter subsidy might be the appropriate response, according to second-best analysis. So, under this concept at least, two wrongs can make a right.

This explains why the United States has pursued a policy of first negotiating international agreements to limit or eliminate subsidies, then offsetting them with countervailing duties, and finally using counter subsidies occasionally. Since the United States has chosen for a variety of reasons (good reasons in the author's view) not to engage in sweeping subsidization, a policy of both reaching international agreements to eliminate subsidies and offsetting subsidies with countervailing duties is fundamentally sound. If subsidies can someday be eliminated or, perhaps, limited to instances in which they may serve recognized objectives without distorting trade, countervailing duties or counter subsidies may become unnecessary. Until that happens, however, both U.S. strategies are critical in combating what has become an increasingly serious international trade problem.

Notes

1. *Final Texts of the GATT Uruguay Round Agreement,* "Agreement on Subsidies and Countervailing Measures," Part IV: Non-Actionable Subsidies, Article 8.

2. Further reading on steel and agricultural subsidies can be found in Robert L. Paarlberg, *Fixing Farm Trade: Policy Options for the United States* (Cambridge, MA: Ballinger Publishing, 1988); Thomas R. Howell, William A. Noellert, Jesse G. Kreier and Alan Wm. Wolff, *Steel and the State* (Boulder, CO: Westview Press, 1988).

3. See Clyde Prestowitz, *Trading Places: How We Allowed Japan to Take the Lead* (New York, NY.: Basic Books, 1988); and Laura D'Andrea Tyson, *Who's Bashing Whom? Trade Conflict in High-Technology Industries* (Washington, DC: Institute for International Economics, 1992).

Chapter Eighteen
Case Studies

The preceding discussion of the economic case for combating subsidies from a U.S. policy perspective may at times seem too theoretical. To understand better the problems subsidies have caused in key industrial sectors, and the challenges U.S. policy faces in combating them, three specific case studies have been selected: 1) civilian aerospace, 2) steel, and 3) forest products. The selection of these case studies should not be taken to mean that these are the only sectors where subsidies are present or that they suffer most from subsidies. These three examples, however, are generally typical of the dimensions of the subsidy challenge.

Civilian Aerospace: Airbus

Airbus Industrie of Europe is a consortium of airplane manufacturers responsible for one of the most successful entries into a high-tech, high-investment industry. In the course of twenty years, Airbus has been able to make sales accounting for nearly half of the global market in some years, and it now ranks right behind the United States' Boeing Corporation.[1] Airbus's quick rise in a hard-to-enter sector previously dominated by the United States is due to massive subsidies from the richest of the European countries: Germany, France, Great Britain, and Spain. Since its inception, Airbus has received approximately $13–14 billion in direct subsidies and below-market-rate loans (1970–90),[2] and, as a result, it has been free to invest in new technologies and offer excellent financing deals for its customers. Concurrently, one U.S. aerospace manufacturer has departed the civilian aircraft business, and another has been losing ground for the past ten years: Lockheed and McDonnell-Douglas, respectively (McDonnell-Douglas recovered some ground in 1995). While these American companies offered (and, in one case, continues to offer) competitive products, they have not had the financial ability to invest in new products or to expand their product line greatly and compete on an even footing with a company that essentially is protected from failure.

The importance of the aerospace industry to America cannot be overstated. In 1993, aircraft and equipment exports were valued at over $31 billion, or about 6 percent of total U.S. exports.[3] Boeing alone employs 120,000 people, with an additional 540,000 indirectly employed in generally high-paying jobs through Boeing production; and this number is down significantly from the late 1980s.[4] Even with Airbus competition, civil aircraft sales in the next twenty years are expected to generate $1 trillion.[5] The importance of the industry to the future of the United States is obvious, and thus it is crucial that there be fair competition in the civilian aerospace industry.

The Rise of Airbus

In 1970, the world commercial aircraft market was dominated by the American companies—Boeing, McDonnell-Douglas, and Lockheed. Around this time, Germany and France joined in an effort to challenge the United States directly in this lucrative market. In 1970, Airbus Consortium was formed as a GIE (Groupement d' Interet Economique—an entity that, under French law, does not have to disclose financial information) with the intention to enter the short-to-medium-range flight market. Shortly after, the United Kingdom and Spain joined the venture, which was then composed of four mainly government-owned aircraft companies: Aerospatiale of France, Deutsche Airbus of Germany, British Aerospace, and CASA of Spain. With a massive infusion of start-up funds, Airbus was able to devise the first twin-engine, wide-body plane, the A300, which was delivered in 1974. Airbus's R&D costs came from the partner governments:[6] 38 percent from Germany, 38 percent from France, 20 percent from the United Kingdom, and 4 percent from Spain.[7] While the threat to U.S. aircraft manufacturers seemed small at the time, there was some expressed concern about the level of government support for Airbus, and that concern persisted during the Tokyo Round of multilateral negotiations in which a General Agreement on Trade in Aircraft was developed and signed.

During the 1980s, the world aircraft market boomed. Between 1985 and 1990, with continuing strong support from the member governments, Airbus was able to introduce two other models: one smaller than the original A300 (the A320) and another with long-range capacity (the A310). Airbus was well on its way to developing a full product line. In 1989, it overtook McDonnell-Douglas in value of sales, a lead it has maintained. Boeing is still in control of the long-range market but has had to compete aggressively with Airbus.

Some of the new technology used in the civilian aircraft industry during the 1990s was originally developed by Airbus, which had the luxury of continual inputs for research and development, and which was not required to repay the parent governments. The four countries involved have shielded Airbus from market forces and downturns in the civil aircraft market and allowed it to remain cutting-edge in the development of next-generation technology.

The Civil Aircraft Code, 1979

During the 1970s, there was little concern in the United States over the fledgling Airbus, and it was not until 1978 that the U.S. House of Representatives held hearings on subsidies in the aerospace industry. Although one of the highlights of the Tokyo Round of multilateral negotiations (1976–79) was the Subsidies Code, which grew out of numerous complaints from the United States about subsidies, trade in aircraft was subject to a separate code, the GATT Agreement on Trade in Civil Aircraft.

The GATT Agreement on Trade in Civil Aircraft, also known as the Civil Aircraft Code, was signed on April 12, 1979, by the United States, Austria, Belgium, Canada, Denmark, West Germany, France, Ireland, Italy, Japan, Luxembourg, Netherlands, Norway, Romania, Sweden, Switzerland, and the United Kingdom. The code established a

Committee on Trade in Civil Aircraft for oversight of aircraft disputes and eliminated import duties on commercial aircraft. It included governmental assurances that airlines could select aircraft on a competitive basis, subject only to limited trade restrictions. Government subsidies were not prohibited specifically in the code, but a commitment was made to a pricing mechanism that would take into account "reasonable expectations for reimbursements of all costs." Also, the Aircraft Code stated in general terms that the Subsidies Code covered trade in civil aircraft. All in all, the Aircraft Code was more a market-opening agreement to ensure free trade, than a discipline on subsidies.

In 1984 and 1985, as Airbus was growing, gaining new customers, and expanding its product line, the U.S. government grew more concerned and initiated discussions with the European Commission on aircraft subsidies. As a result, the Large Aircraft Sector Understanding was signed at the GATT, modifying the 1979 agreement and attempting to regulate customer financing for aircraft purchases by using interest rates rather than government financial assistance.

The Civil Aircraft Code currently has twenty-two signatories, and plans have been under way to amend it with the bilateral agreement signed in 1992 by the United States and European Union. A final agreement between the two governments has yet to be made.

The United States–European Community Dispute at the GATT

By 1986 serious talks on aircraft subsidies had already been under way for more than a year between the two governments. The United States argued that subsidies to Airbus protected it from risk and provided funds for development and export financing, as well as direct export and sales subsidies. Europe countered that its subsidies were necessary to compete with the heavy infusion of military money into the U.S. aerospace industry and also to compete against a near monopoly in the industry. The European claim was that the U.S. government subsidized its aircraft industry, just less directly, through extensive military research and development that was then transferred to the civilian sector. From the United States' point of view, the level and range of military involvement was not comparable with the commitment of the European governments to develop the strongest civil aircraft manufacturer in the world. U.S. government support for military research is not regular, or guaranteed, and is nothing more than a simple commercial purchase of aircraft for military use, not a subsidy. The U.S. government also mandates repayment of any technology used in commercial endeavors developed under government contract. More important, in the United States, decision making and investment in the aircraft sector is driven by commercial competition, whereas in Europe, at least in the aircraft sector, the basis for civilian aircraft development has been a targeted, government industrial policy.

In 1987, Congress held hearings on Airbus, and President Reagan made several motions that Section 301 might be used against Europe because of subsidies to Airbus that were in violation of trade agreements and that caused harm to a vital American industry. Talks were held at the GATT, and there was great effort to resolve the dispute, but each government continued to justify its actions by pointing to the other government's support for its industry. From 1988 to 1991, major trade action was often threatened against Airbus by the U.S. government (sanctions, etc.), but each time, a recommitment to negotiations was made, and official trade action was deferred. In 1991, both countries agreed to limit government support to 45 percent of total costs, but U.S. officials continued to push for a 25 percent limit. Transparency continued to be a major issue in the negotiations, and Airbus was encouraged to make its subsidies and financial records public.

In 1989, a deal was made between the German government and Daimler Benz to allow acquisition of Deutsche Airbus in an effort to privatize. Included in the deal was a promise by the German government to cover losses caused by fluctuation in exchange rates (if the dollar fell below DM 1.6). This type of backing was valuable, especially since the dollar was depreciating and it was becoming increasingly cheaper to manufacture in the United States.

Once this agreement was approved by the European Commission, the United States, still struggling with the general problem of direct government subsidies to Airbus, chose to file a formal complaint against the EC based on this guarantee. In 1990, the United States requested consultations at the GATT Subsidies Committee (the committee that oversaw the Subsidies Code), claiming that the exchange-rate guarantee was in effect an export subsidy. Additional problems stemmed from the desire of the European Commission to resolve this dispute in the Civil Aircraft Committee, while the United States insisted that it be handled in the Subsidies Committee—the rate guarantee was a more direct violation of the Subsidies Code in this case, and thus a better forum for the United States' claim.

Consultations at the GATT did not resolve the dispute, and a dispute settlement panel was formed. In 1992, the dispute panel at the Subsidies Committee ruled in favor of the United States against the Germans, stating that the exchange-rate guarantee was, in essence, an export subsidy and a violation of the Subsidies Code.[8] The decision was blocked by the EC. Shortly after, Germany dropped the guarantee but not before contributing a large amount to each aircraft completed during 1990.

Government consultations on the general subsidy issue for aircraft continued throughout this specific dispute. The United States, originally opposed to any allowable government subsidy level for development, was willing to concede to 25 percent support. The EC refused to go lower than 40–45percent. In July of 1992, an agreement, the U.S.-EU Agreement concerning the Application of the GATT Agreement on Trade in Civil Aircraft, was signed, covering financial support for large aircraft (100+ seats). This agreement prohibited support for production, marketing, and sales and limited subsidies to 33 percent of cost for development, with mandatory repayment including interest. Included was a limit on indirect government support, 3 percent of industry sales, or 4 percent for any one firm for the products covered. The bilateral agreement also provided for increased transparency by requiring details on the amount of government research and support for the industry. Finally, the agreement included more specific provisions for trade in aircraft to comply with the Subsidies Agreement of the new World Trade Organization (WTO Agreement on Subsidies and Countervailing Measures).[9]

While this agreement was significant, and held off the United States from launching another dispute settlement panel, further discussions have been held since, and, at the close of the Uruguay Round negotiations, Civil Aircraft remained unresolved.

Recent Developments

The bilateral agreement signed in 1992 between the EU and the United States has not yet been incorporated into the Civil Aircraft Code for approval by the other twenty signatories of the code. This issue was one of the two items left pending during the Uruguay Round negotiations, with the expectation that adjustments to the agreement would be made in 1994. Throughout 1994, negotiations continued, with the intention to expand the agreement.

The Clinton administration has expressed dissatisfaction with the European Union's compliance with the agreement, as well as a strong desire to lower the level of allowable subsidies from the 1992 level of 33 percent to 25 percent.

On the European side, there have been complaints as well. Europe has complained about a July 1994 contract between NASA and Boeing/McDonnell-Douglas, worth $440 million, for the study of high-speed civil transport.[10] The French government was also extremely concerned about the decline of the dollar's exchange rate in 1995 and its impact on the civil aircraft market.

While there are many issues in the civilian aircraft debate, it is almost impossible to ignore the huge market distortion caused by European subsidies to Airbus. In recent years, through much negotiation by the United States, some progress has been made, and Airbus will be paying back some funds to the parent governments. Meanwhile, Airbus has used subsidies to establish a strong competitive position in this sector. This has cost the United States one civil aircraft company, greatly harmed another, and generally caused the loss of tens of thousands of jobs in the aerospace sector. Without a doubt, Airbus subsidies have done more direct damage to U.S. industry than any other industrial subsidy, and the slow U.S. response has allowed irreparable damage to be done to the U.S. competitive position in the aerospace sector. Though it is impossible to be precise, there can be little question that a large percentage of the thousands of jobs lost in this sector over the last ten years are a direct or indirect result of Airbus subsidies.

Steel

Over the past forty years, the U.S. steel industry has gone from being world leader to near death, to massive restructuring, and finally back to a competitive position. The difficulties faced by the U.S. steel companies are unique in that they have had to compete with foreign steel companies receiving massive government subsidies, in both U.S. and foreign markets, and to weather a period of world overcapacity that also contributed to large-scale dumping in the relatively open U.S. market. The survival of the industry is due, in large part, to intervention by the U.S. government in the 1980s and 1990s, utilizing a wide range of U.S. trade laws and international agreements to stave off unfair competition from around the world.

Steel products engender the most frequently cited of all countervailing duty and antidumping cases. The importance of steel to the country has been and continues to be critical: the industry employed 163,000 people in 1987.[11] The high number of antidumping and countervailing duty cases can be attributed to subsidized competition from dozens of European and Asian countries, which have spent considerable amounts to build and maintain steel industries and to protect them during business-cycle downturns. This type of support was generally lacking in the United States, and thus the U.S. steel industry was devastated by subsidies and dumping in the 1970s and early 1980s.

As world sales slowed in the 1980s, European and Japanese governments attempted to help their industries weather the readjustment with subsidies. Steel subsidies in Europe alone, between 1980 and 1985, reached $37 billion.[12] At the same time, other industrializing countries were building overcapacity and then dumping in the United States market.

It was not until the 1980s that the U.S. government actively intervened in the industry. In 1981, the Reagan administration initiated seven antidumping and countervailing duty cases.[13] In 1982, Section 301 cases were initiated against various European countries, claiming they were in violation of the GATT Subsidies Code.[14] The steel industry itself, in 1982, filed 132 antidumping petitions against foreign steel.[15] In 1984, as a resolution to the 301 cases, the U.S. trade representative requested that the ITC initiate a Section 201 case

(Section 201, the "escape clause" under U.S. trade law and the GATT, allows industries to file for protection from a substantial increase in imports causing serious injury to the industry). In the Trade and Tariff Act of 1984, Congress specifically mentioned the steel problem and gave the president power to impose quotas to protect the industry. Later in 1984, the ITC's decision on the 201 case recommended a five-year plan of quotas and tariffs to protect the industry. Although the ITC ruled in favor of the industry, the Reagan administration, concerned that such measures would jeopardize trade relations with the respective countries, instead offered voluntary import restrictions to a number of the respondents in the cases.[16]

Voluntary restraint agreements (VRAs) were made with seven key steel-exporting countries: Australia, Brazil, Japan, Mexico, South Africa, South Korea, and Spain. Once a country made an agreement, the unfair trade case against it was withdrawn. Additional unfair trade cases led nineteen additional countries to negotiate VRAs with the United States.[17]

The next year, imported steel peaked at 26.2 percent of the U.S. steel market.[18] Under the VRAs, President Reagan's intention had been to lower imports of steel to 18 percent of total finished steel sales, but, because certain countries refused to enter into agreements, and because of an increase in new countries exporting steel to the United States, the percentage of steel imports remained high for the next year. By 1989, however, steel imports had fallen, and in 1991 steel imports were down to 15.9 percent.[19]

In 1992, President Bush did not renew the voluntary restraint agreements, due to a stronger steel market and a renewed commitment by the administration and the steel industry to employ the trade laws as they were meant by Congress to be used.[20] Later that year, a large number of dumping and subsidies petitions against steel exporters in Europe and Asia were filed. In 1993, the Commerce Department ruled in favor of the U.S. industry against twelve countries for subsidies and against nineteen countries for dumping.[21]

The competitive position of the U.S. steel industry has become something of a Rorschach test of international trade—each observer sees it as proof of his or her favorite theory. Some see it as a case study of a politically powerful and inefficient industry exercising undue influence. Others see it as illustration of weakness of U.S. trade laws.

There are elements of truth in both of these views. The U.S. steel industry did cause some of its own competitive problems, but foreign subsidization and other unfair practices were also major factors. Whatever the case, the level of government intervention in the steel market—sparked largely by subsidies—is strong evidence that subsidization has the effect of breeding even more serious market distortions.

Forest Products

The forest products sector may not initially come to mind in the context of subsidies, but lumber from Canada has been the target of the largest U.S. countervailing duty case to date, affecting $14 billion in trade annually.[22] The Canadian lumber case is notable for two reasons. First, it involves, as briefly noted previously, an innovative method for delivering the subsidy. Second, the lumber cases have involved considerable international dispute settlement, which raises important questions about future use of U.S. trade laws and potential conflict with international dispute settlement.

The Canadian lumber case involves a subsidy conferred without any direct payment to Canadian lumber producers. The Canadian provinces own virtually all of the timberland and provide the right to cut trees—stumpage rights—at a rate below the market price. The difference has narrowed in recent years, but in the mid-1980s, the rate was as little as 10 percent of the price of similar stumpage rights in the U.S. market, which is only a few miles away in some cases. Since the Canadian provinces blocked the export of unprocessed logs, the financial advantage of the subsidy provided was enjoyed by Canadian lumber producers.

The U.S. lumber industry was aware of the existence of stumpage-rights subsidies in Canada for a number of years but first began to focus U.S. government attention on the issue in the early 1980s. In 1983, the U.S. Commerce Department, in a controversial decision, found that Canadian stumpage subsidies were not countervailable, essentially because they did not confer a direct financial benefit.[23] The Commerce Department decision was widely criticized as too narrow and inconsistent with both previous ITA practice and the Subsidies Code. As a result, when the case was brought forward again two years later, the ITA found that the stumpage subsidies constituted a 15 percent countervailable subsidy on Canadian lumber imports into the United States. A Memorandum of Understanding was negotiated between the United States and Canada that served as a suspension agreement. The MOU established a 15 percent export tax that the Canadian federal government collected on timber exports to the United States, with procedures for reviewing provincial efforts to phase out timber subsidies and for reducing the export tax if reform was found.

Some progress has been made over the last ten years to reduce the provincial subsidies, but substantial subsidies remain. For a variety of unique political and economic reasons, Canada exported most of its lumber production to the United States, but with a history of fearing U.S. domination, it was very sensitive to U.S.-Canada trade disputes. The MOU remained a political hot potato in Canada. (Outside of some timber-producing districts, the issue never took on much political importance in the United States.) It was thus a major focus of Canadian trade negotiators in both the U.S.-Canada Free Trade Agreement (FTA) and the Uruguay Round of trade negotiations, although no direct changes in the MOU were negotiated in either forum. The U.S.-Canada FTA did, however, establish a new binational-panel system for adjudicating disputes over the operation of countervailing duty and antidumping laws.[24]

In 1991, Canada unexpectedly and unilaterally withdrew from the MOU. The United States retaliated by reimposing the export tax as a duty, using Section 301, and launching a new countervailing duty case. The new case focused on both the stumpage subsidies and the ban on exports of logs as related, but separate, subsidies. The ITA found a subsidy of 11.5 percent and the ITC found injury. Canada, however, challenged both the subsidy finding and the injury determination under the U.S.-Canada FTA and appealed the retaliatory action under Section 301 to the GATT. The appeals on these issues stretched on for some time. In the end, Canada won on appeal, although every U.S. panelist to hear the issue ruled in favor of the United States (all Canadian panelists ruled in favor of Canada, and the panels had Canadian majorities).

A U.S. judge who sat on the final appeal criticized his Canadian counterparts for rendering the most egregiously wrong "judicial" decision in which he had ever participated. A full discussion of the appeals involved in this case is included in Appendix D, but suffice it to say that the operation of international dispute procedures in this case raises broader issues for the function of U.S. antidumping and countervailing duty laws. It may be that the bilateral nature of this dispute and the acute Canadian nationalism it inspired make it unique, but it is still a case study that should be borne in mind when considering the often complex relationship between U.S. countervailing duty law and international agreements. Though the U.S. duty has been lifted, bilateral consultations on Canadian lumber subsidies continue, and the issue is likely to stretch on for some time.

Notes

1. In July of 1994, Airbus announced that it had received 55 percent of the world's aircraft orders for the first half of that year ("Airbus Captures 55 Percent Market Share in First Half," *Aviation Daily*, July 21, 1994, 116). In 1995, Airbus sales subsequently declined. Given the competitive nature of the industry, substantial, periodic share movement is likely.

2. This figure is from a much cited U.S. Department of Commerce study performed by Gellman Associates. If this amount had been borrowed at commercial rates, the study estimates, it would be double, around $26 billion; Gellman Research Associates, Inc., *An Economic and Financial Review of Airbus Industrie* (Jenkintown, PA: DOC, 1990).

3. Department of Commerce, *U.S. Foreign Trade Highlights* (Washington, DC: DOC, 1993).

4. International Association of Machinists, "America's Last, Great Industry," *IAM Journal*, Winter 1995, 12.

5. John Mintz, "Betting It All on 777; Making a New Jet on Which Its Future Rests, Boeing Remade Itself Too," *Washington Post*, March 26, 1995, H1.

6. Eric Vayle, "Collision Course in Commercial Aircraft," *Harvard Business School* case study, 1991, 7.

7. M.J. Artis and N. Lee, *The Economics of the European Union* (Oxford: Oxford University Press, 1994), 149.

8. "German Exchange Rate Scheme Found to be Export Subsidy for Airbus Parts," *Inside U.S. Trade,* January 24, 1992, 1.

9. U.S. International Trade Commission, *The Year in Trade, 1993, Operations of the Trade Agreements Program* (Washington, DC: ITC, 1993), 30, 46.

10. "Boeing, MDC get $440 Million NASA Contract for HSCT Research," *Aviation Daily*, July 19, 1994, 99.

11. Thomas R. Howell, et al., *Steel and The State* (Boulder, CO: Westview Press, 1988), 503. This number is down from 399,000 employees in the steel industry in 1980.

12. Lawrence Chimerine, et al., *Can the Phoenix Survive? The Fall and the Rise of the American Steel Industry* (Washington, DC: ESI, June 1994), 58–59. The

European countries included are: Belgium, Denmark, Germany, France, Ireland, Italy, Luxembourg, the Netherlands, United Kingdom.

13. Howell, et al., *Steel and the State,* 522.

14. Greg Mastel and Rachel Hines, *Section 301: A Catalyst for Free Trade* (Washington, DC: ESI, 1995), 24.

15. Howell, et al., *Steel and the State*, 522.

16. General Accounting Office, *International Trade: The Health of the U.S. Steel Industry* (Washington, DC: GAO, 1989), 1–6.

17. Howell, et al., *Steel and the State*, 530–531.

18. Ibid., 532.

19. Michael Moskow, "Steel Industry Now Poised to Compete," *American Metals Market,* June 8, 1992.

20. A stronger steel market as defined by higher productivity (person hours per ton), a better quality product, more streamlined plants (smaller, more efficient plants that melt scrap metals, called minimills), and lower prices.

21. Peter Behr, "12 Nations Are Cited on Steel Exports; Preliminary U.S. Ruling Calls Practices Unfair," *Washington Post,* December 1, 1992, B1; Peter Behr, "19 Countries Are Cited for Steel Dumping," *Washington Post*, January 28, 1993, D11.

22. Forest products case history from: Gary Hufbauer and Shelton Erb, *Subsidies in International Trade* (Washington, DC: Institute for International Economics, 1984), 95–97; Coalition for Fair Lumber Imports, *Understanding Canadian Lumber Subsidies* (Washington, D.C.: Dewey Ballantine, 1995).

23. Hufbauer and Erb, *Subsidies*, 96–97.

24. Judith Bello and Alan F. Holmer, *Guide to the U.S.-Canada Free Trade Agreement* (New Jersey: Prentice Hall Law and Business, 1990), 814–15.

Chapter Nineteen

Countering Subsidies under U.S. Law

As is clear from the preceding discussion, the primary U.S. policy tool for countering subsidies is countervailing duty law. Countervailing duty cases are initiated less frequently than antidumping actions and, as the chart of recent cases in Table 19.1 demonstrates, in addition to being less frequent, they are generally directed at imports from a diverse group of countries—different, in many cases, from the countries that are targets of antidumping actions. There are several reasons for this difference.

First, the leading target of antidumping actions is now China. Most dumping complaints against nonmarket economies could be easily pursued as countervailing duty cases since, at their core, they involve state-sponsored trade. The ITA even briefly experimented with handling these cases as countervailing duty complaints but ultimately decided instead to continue handling them under antidumping law. Second, two other prominent targets of antidumping complaints—Japan and Korea—appear much less frequently as targets of countervailing duty investigations. This is likely because these countries seem to prefer providing aid to industries in the form of trade barriers, which are handled as antidumping complaints, not subsidies. The difference in the distribution of the targets of dumping and countervailing duty cases is thus primarily explained by differences in ITA practice and differences in foreign trade practices.

Table 19.1 **Affirmative Determinations in Countervailing Duty Cases, 1985–94, by Country**

	85	86	87	88	89	90	91	92	93	94	TOTAL
Japan											0
Canada	1	2	2		2	2		2	1	2	14
Thailand	2	1	1		2	1	1				8
Brazil	2	2						1	2		7
Germany								1	4		5
New Zealand	2	2	1								5
Korea	1	1	1						1		4
France			1					1	1		3
Mexico	1	1							1		3
United Kingdom								1	2		3
Venezuela				1	1				1		3
Peru	2		1								3
India								1	1		2
Sweden	1								1		2
Turkey		1	1								2
Norway							1	1			2
Spain	1								1		2
Argentina	1			1		1					3
Taiwan			1								1
Italy										1	1
Singapore					1						1
Israel			1								1
Yugoslavia	1										1
Belgium									1		1
Ecuador		1									1
Malaysia				1							1
Saudi Arabia		1									1
Iran		1									1
Sri Lanka	1										1
Austria	1										1

Source: U.S. International Trade Commission.

As in the case with antidumping investigations, some critics complain that the ITA is biased against foreign interests in the application of countervailing duty laws. An extensive discussion of this issue is included in the antidumping section of this book, part II, but a few points are worth emphasizing in regard to countervailing duty laws. The ITA does make a higher percentage of affirmative subsidy findings than the ITC makes affirmative injury findings, though the disparity is somewhat smaller than in antidumping cases. There are two primary reasons for this disparity. First, petitioning industries normally have a much better idea of whether they are facing an unfair subsidy than they have of whether they can pass the injury test. The standards for subsidies are clearly articulated by U.S. law and expanded upon by the ITA, whereas the criteria for deciding material injury at the ITC is always less clear, dependent on future economic events outside the control of the industry, and subject to substantial change as the membership of the ITC changes. Second, the preliminary injury decision by the ITC, and consultation with the industry, kills many poor countervailing duty cases before they ever reach the ITA.

Further, allegations of systematic bias overlook the main point that the U.S. process is transparent and provides opportunities for input from both sides at all stages in the proceeding, a great improvement over the much less transparent practices that many other countries follow. As is the case with antidumping decisions, all ITA countervailing duty decisions are subject to review by U.S. courts, the new World Trade Organization and, in some instances, NAFTA authorities. After decades of study and improvements in procedures, countervailing duty laws now function relatively smoothly. Certainly, occasional errors are made, but built-in checks throughout the system address systematic error.

Countervailing duty law, however, is not a perfect tool for the job of countering subsidies. It has three major weaknesses. First, it can be employed only after the fact and, because of the injury test, only after the subsidies have already caused significant trade distortions. Second, as is the case with European agriculture and aerospace subsidies, subsidies—both export and production—may have their primary effect in third markets, rather than the U.S. market, and thus cannot be fully addressed with countervailing duties in the U.S. market. Finally, as briefly noted above, the primary effect of domestic production subsidies may well be in the home market of the subsidizer; this has certainly been the case, again, with certain European agricultural subsidies, such as oilseeds. Countervailing duties cannot even be applied in this case since the subsidized product is never exported. Broadening the definition of a subsidy to cover upstream subsidies can, in some instances, make countervailing duties more relevant, but they are still an imperfect tool.

The most obvious alternate approach potentially available under U.S. law is to impose countervailing subsidies on domestic production to offset the effect of foreign subsidies. This option has even received some discussion in the GATT. The United States has never adopted a systematic approach to extending counter-subsidies, but such actions have occasionally been explored on an ad hoc basis. For example, in the mid-1980s, a program known as the Export Enhancement Program (EEP) was created to provide export subsidies on U.S. agricultural products facing subsidized competition—primarily from Europe. The U.S. Export Import Bank has a $200 million war chest to counter subsidized export financing by the United States' competitors.[1] The Export Import Bank is also committed to matching foreign offers of subsidized financing. Additionally, legislation was considered in the U.S. Congress to extend subsidies to the U.S. aerospace industry in order to counter Airbus.

This approach, however, has a number of limitations. For example, it obviously can be very costly. Although counter subsidies would have less impact on consumers, their impact on taxpayers could be substantial. The U.S. government has been willing as a matter of policy to commit to automatic imposition of duties in order to counter subsidies when injurious subsidies are detected. It is difficult to imagine a similar blanket commitment to spend whatever it takes to provide counter subsidies. Further, counter subsidies also run the risk of starting an escalating subsidy competition that could involve additional countries.

The United States has also used its broadest trade law—Section 301—in efforts to counter subsidies. As described earlier, Section 301 was used to impose duties on subsidized Canadian lumber when Canada broke the MOU with the United States on lumber subsidies. The most frequent early use of Section 301 was, in fact, to challenge European agricultural subsidies—especially to counteract their effect in third markets and within Europe. Generally, these efforts were unsuccessful because they were hampered by ineffective GATT dispute settlement procedures and an unwillingness by U.S. administrations to pursue cases forcefully. Section 301 was moderately successful in challenging the European practice of replacing trade barriers with subsidies.[2]

Section 301 is broadly targeted to address any problem that "burdens or restricts U.S. commerce." In practice, however, it has been used chiefly to counter trade problems affecting exports; import problems have been left to antidumping and countervailing duty law. This means Section 301 is likely to be employed only when subsidies restrict U.S. exports.

Notes

1. U.S. Trade Promotion Coordinating Committee, "Report to the U.S. Congress," *National Export Strategy* (Washington, DC: DOC, October 1994), 108.

2. A detailed listing of these cases and an analysis of successes in combating agricultural subsidies is found in Greg Mastel and Rachel Hines, *Section 301: A Catalyst for Free Trade* (Washington, DC: ESI, 1995).

Chapter Twenty

Countering Subsidies under International Law

Limitations on subsidies have been discussed in a number of international forums, and bilateral and regional forums have attempted to limit subsidies in some cases. The most notable success in this regard has been within the European Union, which has imposed substantial limits on the use of subsidies by its member states. Multilaterally, both the G-7 and the OECD have focused on subsidies, the OECD having carefully monitored subsidies over a period of many years. Through studies, it has drawn attention to problems caused by export and agricultural subsidies. It has also established certain guidelines on the use of subsidies, including subsidized export-financing by OECD members.[1]

The OECD has generally functioned, however, as a forum for intellectual discussion, not as an enforcer of commitments. Instead, the concepts developed by the OECD have generally been given form in the context of GATT agreements. Countervailing duty laws had already been in use for decades in many countries before the GATT came into existence. Therefore, from its inception, the GATT recognized the importance of subsidies as trade problems, and subsidies are, in part, the focus of three major GATT Articles—VI, XVI, and XXIII. The treatment was hardly comprehensive, however. In essence, the GATT endorsed the operation of countervailing duty laws to counter subsidies and noted that subsidies could cause trade problems in certain instances.

The GATT's 1979 Code on Subsidies and Countervailing Measures—normally referred to as the Subsidies Code—greatly elaborated upon these initial GATT provisions. The Subsidies Code, though it was voluntary and not adopted by many GATT members, was significant in several regards. First, as noted, it defined some subsidies, basically export subsidies, as violations of the GATT subject to dispute settlement.[2] Export subsidies for agricultural products and other basic products were permissible if they were not used to gain more than "an equitable share of the world market."[3] GATT panels were unable to give much meaning to the "equitable share" language, essentially making agricultural export subsidies subject to no restriction, but the disciplines on other direct export subsidies were the first step toward meaningful subsidy discipline.

The Subsidies Code provided one other major change in the enforcement of countervailing duty laws, by requiring the application of the injury test before countervailing duties could be imposed on the subsidies of another signatory to the Subsidies Code.[4] This initially seems a step backward, and it may, in fact, be a step backward. Why should it be necessary to pass the injury test before subsidies can be countervailed? After all, if the subsidy distorts trade, shouldn't it be countered regardless? This argument is persuasive. However, the counter argument is that the injury test is the quid pro quo for convincing certain countries to forswear export subsidies. The United States and other, early Subsidies Code members used the injury test in this way. Imports from nonsignatories were countervailed without an injury test, imports from signatories were subject to the injury test. This convinced several countries—notably, from the U.S. perspective, Mexico—to sign the Subsidies Code.

The 1979 Subsidies Code also continued the GATT practice of granting "special and differential" treatment to developing countries. Thus, developing countries were effectively exempt from much of the subsidy discipline.[5]

The GATT included no more major reforms related to subsidies until the Uruguay Round of GATT negotiations, which ended in 1994. The major innovation of the Uruguay Round was that the new Subsidies Agreement was integrated into the core of the GATT agreement—i.e., no longer was it just a voluntary, side agreement. All members of the GATT (now WTO) must accept subsidy discipline.

The second major change established in the new Subsidies Agreement was binding dispute settlement. Following previous GATT practice, subsidy-related dispute settlement panels could be blocked by any member country, including the country maintaining the practice at issue. This rendered it an ineffectual dispute settlement body; the situation was analogous to a defendant in a criminal trial being able to block a guilty verdict. The new agreement, following practice throughout most of the Uruguay Round Agreement, allows decision-making panels to be blocked only by consensus of all member countries, including the country bringing the complaint. The time lines for dispute settlement are also tighter; a complaint of the Subsidies Agreement violation must be resolved within 225 days after it is filed, or 285 days if appealed.

Another major, positive innovation was to provide increased discipline on certain classes of subsidies. Subsidies contingent upon export performance, or upon the use of domestic goods over imported goods, are banned outright, and an extensive, illustrative list of prohibited subsidies was included in the agreement. Building upon the 1979 Code, three other broad groups of subsidies are generally prohibited: 1) subsidies that injure the domestic industry of another member country, 2) subsidies that nullify or impair trade concessions elsewhere granted, and 3) subsidies that seriously prejudice the interests of another member country.[6] Serious prejudice is defined as: 1) ad valorem subsidization exceeding 5 percent; 2) subsidies to cover operating losses sustained by an industry; 3) subsidies to cover operating losses by an enterprise, unless applied as a one-time measure to provide time for the development of long-term solutions and to avoid acute social problems; or 4) direct forgiveness of debt and grants to cover debt repayment.[7]

If a country can establish in its complaint that any of the criteria for serious prejudice is met, a presumption is established against the subsidizing country that can be rebutted by establishing that the subsidy has none of the following harmful effects: 1) displacing or impeding imports, 2) displacing exports of other member countries in third markets, 3) causing significant price undercutting or lost sales by another member country, and 4) increasing world market share of the subsidizing country in a subsidized primary product/commodity.[8]

Although substantial deference is still granted to developing countries, the new Subsidies Agreement also phases out or phases down some of the effective exemptions developing countries have historically enjoyed under the Subsidies Code.[9] Taken together, these changes are likely to make the Subsidies Agreement a stronger tool than its predecessor in combating subsidies directly.

Other provisions in the Subsidies Agreement tend to cut against the policing of subsidies, however. The agreement expands the list of permissible, or green, subsidies in three new areas: 1) subsidies for pre-competitive research and development, 2) regional development, and 3) installation of environmental protection technology.[10] Each of these green areas included a number of restrictions aimed at ensuring that the category of subsidies allowed was not expanded. In theory, each of these permissible categories is allowable, since they all aim to redress serious social or environmental market failings, not to distort international trade. Especially now that other forms of subsidies are subject to increased discipline, however, attempts are likely to be made to expand these new permissible subsidy categories to allow broader, and potentially more objectionable, subsidies than the agreements framers intended. Only time will tell if the integrity of the exemptions can be maintained.

The new Subsidies Agreement also includes many procedural changes in the determination of such issues as standing, injury, definition of injury and, as previously discussed, definition of a countervailable subsidy. There was considerable concern initially that these changes would weaken U.S. countervailing duty law. For the most part, however, the procedural changes do not require major changes in U.S. law. The new Subsidies Agreement will require petitioners to prove some additional points but, according to most practitioners, seem likely to change the outcome of only a few cases. Many of the procedural changes affecting countervailing duty law are the same as those made with regard to antidumping law and are discussed in Appendix D. Four changes are worthy of separate note:

Sunset. As is the case with antidumping orders, countervailing duty orders are sunset (lifted) after five years unless evidence is provided that lifting the order would likely result in continued injury from subsidized competition.[11]

De Minimis Subsidy Levels. De Minimis levels for subsidies are established at 1 percent for developed countries[12] and 2 percent for developing countries.[13] Developing countries that phase out export subsidies ahead of schedule will be subject to a 3 percent de minimis subsidy level.[14]

Developing Countries. The new Subsidies Agreement establishes no minimum level of imports for developed countries to be subject to countervailing duties. For developing countries, subsidized exports are exempt if they account for less than 4 percent of total imports, unless the collective share of imports from such countries is greater than 9 percent.[15]

The long-standing U.S. practice of cumulating imports from a number of countries that subsidize their production, in order to determine injury, was formally endorsed by the Subsidies Agreement.[16]

Agriculture. Finally, agriculture was explicitly exempted from all of the subsidy disciplines just described, but the agreement separately provides for significant cuts in both agricultural export and production subsidies.[17] This falls far short of the original U.S. goals for the agricultural portion of these negotiations—the Reagan and Bush administrations had articulated as a goal the virtual elimination of trade-distorting subsidies in the agricultural sector. There are, however, plans for negotiations on further cuts once the initial round of subsidy cuts are fully implemented.

Subsidies have also been the subject of some discussion in negotiations on the NAFTA and its predecessor, the U.S.-Canada FTA. The major innovation in this regard, however, was the establishment of special dispute settlement panels. No other significant subsidy-related provisions have emerged from these negotiations.

Notes

1. Organization for Economic Cooperation and Development, *Arrangement on Guidelines for Officially Supported Export Credits* (Washington, DC: OECD, July 6, 1982).

2. *Final Texts of the GATT Uruguay Round Agreements,* "Agreement on Subsidies and Countervailing Measures," Part I, Article 8.
3. Ibid., Part I, Article 10(2)(a).
4. Ibid., Part I, Article 6.
5. Ibid., Part III, Article 14.
6. *Final Texts of the GATT Uruguay Round Agreements,* "Agreement on Subsidies and Countervailing Measures," Part III: Actionable Subsidies, Article 5 (a)(b)(c).
7. Ibid., Article 6.1(a)(b)(c)(d).
8. Ibid., Article 6.2, 6.3(a)(b)(c)(d).
9. Ibid., Part VIII: Developing Country Members, Article 27.
10. Ibid., Part IV: Non-Actionable Subsidies, Article 8.1, 8.2(a)(b)(c).
11. Ibid., Part V: Countervailing Measures, Article 21.3.
12. Ibid., Article 11.9.
13. Ibid., Part VIII: Developing Country Members, Article 27.10(a).
14. Ibid., Article 27.11.
15. Ibid., Part VIII: Developing Country Members, Article 27.10(b).
16. Ibid., Part V: Countervailing Measures, Article 15.3.
17. Ibid., "Agreement on Agriculture," Part IV, Article 6, Article 9.

Chapter Twenty-One

Conclusions

The new Subsidies Agreement has the potential to increase subsidy discipline. Initially, both proponents and opponents of strong subsidy discipline expressed the view that the new Subsidies Code could decrease discipline. These concerns seem overstated. Most of the procedural changes in the operation of U.S. countervailing duty law were operationalized in U.S. legislation in a manner that minimized the changes in U.S. countervailing duty procedures. The final impact on U.S. countervailing duty law will not be known until the outcome of Subsidies Code dispute settlement panels is known, years hence, but a careful analysis would indicate that only marginal changes are likely.

The new green categories for subsidies may pose greater risks, but, at their core, they strive to define subsidies that legitimately should be permissible. There is reason for concern that exemptions will be broadened and abused by those countries that seek to continue subsidizing. The exemptions include specific language to limit their scope. Again, however, the ultimate impact of these provisions will only be known when the new Subsidies Agreement has been in place for a time and the rulings of dispute settlement panels can be evaluated. In the meantime, monitoring the potential abuse of these exemptions should be a high priority for U.S. trade policy.

To its credit, the new Subsidies Agreement does provide significantly increased discipline of subsidies in a number of regards. If these provisions function as intended, they should significantly increase discipline on subsidies in the future. If they prove effective, nonsubsidizing countries, and industries adversely impacted by subsidies, may turn to these new subsidy disciplines to eliminate subsidies, in addition to using countervailing duties to offset their effect. Most observers, regardless of their views on subsidies and countervailing duties, would see this as a positive development. In economic terms, it involves switching from second-best solutions to a direct elimination of the problem.

The United States should continue a policy of combating subsidies aggressively. The Clinton administration, when it sought provisions in the new Subsidies Agreement to allow certain limited research and development subsidies, was criticized in some circles for departing from consistent U.S. policy in recent decades.[1] The subsidies the administration sought to protect are not likely to have a significant trade distorting effect, and they may well constitute a legitimate instance of government acting to protect subsidies that reflect positive externalities from precommercial R&D, which benefit society.

There is, however, a legitimate basis for challenging the strategic choices of the administration in this instance. Historically, the United States has been unwilling to commit resources to subsidies at the same level as its trading partners. In the current budget debate, this trend seems to be continuing; there is a good prospect that the very programs the administration sought to protect will be eliminated by budget cutters. As a nonsubsidizer, the United States must give careful thought to the wisdom of opening potential new holes in subsidy discipline, holes that are likely to be aggressively exploited and even abused by U.S. trading partners while the United States is reluctant to take full advantage of them. In combating subsidies, the United States must make a fundamental choice: Is the objective to achieve a world in which subsidies are sharply curtailed, or one in which U.S. subsidies are permanently increased? Wavering between those two diametrically opposed objectives makes it unlikely that either will be achieved.

The United States should continue to seek further international discipline on subsidies while continuing aggressive domestic legislation to combat their injurious effects. Unfortunately, as other, more traditional, trade barriers are phased out, there has been a tendency to replace those trade barriers with subsidies. Based on OECD records, there is little evidence that the overall level of subsidies has increased. As other trade distortions are eliminated, however, the economic impact of subsidies—even if they remain at current levels—could be greater. Without tariffs and quotas to blunt the impact of subsidies, the United States could feel their effects more strongly. For this reason, the European Community—now European Union—increased its disciplines on subsidies when the barriers between the member states were eliminated.[2]

This all suggests that the United States may want to be increasingly aggressive in seeking disciplines on subsidies. A further multilateral trade negotiation to expand the GATT now seems years away, but, in the interim, the United States has an ambitious work plan for regional free trade agreements. Discipline on subsidies should be given increased priority in those negotiations, particularly if they include further restrictions on the operation of U.S. countervailing duty law.

Unfortunately, further international discipline on subsidies is likely some years away. Until such discipline emerges, the United States must be prepared to continue countering subsidies with U.S. countervailing duty law and, perhaps also, with counter subsidies in selected instances. Unless the United States continues to combat subsidies aggressively, its industries will be vulnerable to competition from countries that are more willing to subsidize aggressively. Further, unless the United States is willing to fight trading partners' subsidies, these countries are likely to succeed, making them less willing to accept subsidy discipline. The progress the United States made in curtailing agricultural subsidies during the Uruguay Round was due in large part, in the estimation of most observers, to the existence of the Export Enhancement Program, which provided export subsidies for U.S. agricultural exports. By "fighting fire with fire" in the agricultural sector, the United States convinced trading partners of the wisdom of limiting subsidies. It may need to take similar steps in other areas in order to win further agreements.

Notes

1. *Final Texts of the GATT Uruguay Round Agreements*, "Agreement on Subsidies and Countervailing Measures," Part IV: Non-Actionable Subsidies,

Article 8; and John C. Danforth, "Trade Accord Should Be Renegotiated," *St. Louis Post-Dispatch,* February 13, 1994, 3B.

2. The United States may at some point want to consider further disciplines on internal state and local subsidies.

Appendix A

Section 301 Cases

Dates: 1974–April 1996

#	Country Filed Against	Sector	Specific Product	Date	Summary
1	Guatemala	Services	shipping	7/75 to 6/76	Delta Steamship Lines filed a petition against a Guatemalan government decree that required duty-free imports to be brought into Guatemala on Guatemalan carriers, and concurrently filed a case with the Federal Maritime Commission. A tentative agreement was reached and the case was dropped, but the FMC continued the investigation and even threatened retaliation until the decree was revoked.
2	Canada	Agriculture	eggs	7/75 to 3/76	U.S. egg producers filed a petition against Canada's quotas on eggs (and also filed a dumping case against eggs being dumped in the United States by Canadian producers). A working group at the GATT was formed, and through bilateral negotiations, Canada agreed to double its egg quotas. In addition, egg imports to the United States dropped.
3	E.C.	Agriculture	egg albumin (dried egg whites)	8/75 to 1/79	Seymour Foods, Inc., filed a petition against levies imposed by the EC on egg albumin, and the USTR held consultations that eventually led to the elimination of the levy (conversely, import charges were increased, but with the removal of the original levy, exports to the EC grew).
4	E.C.	Agriculture	canned fruits and vegetables	9/75 to 1/79	The National Canners Association filed a petition against import restrictions on canned fruits and vegetables. A GATT panel was formed and found that the EC was in violation of the GATT. The EC removed the restrictions but then replaced them with a subsidy to the canned fruit and vegetable processors.
5	E.C.	Agriculture	malt	11/75 to 6/80	The Great Western Malting Company filed a petition against European subsidies to malt producers, who they claimed had acquired much of the Japanese and world malt market. Through negotiations, the EC eventually reduced the amount of the subsidy.

155

6	E.C.	Agriculture	wheat flour	12/75 to 1/83	The Millers National Federation filed a petition against European subsidies given to wheat flour exporters, which they claimed during the late 70s allowed the EC to win over 50% of the wheat market in the world. The case was brought to the GATT under the recently completed Subsidies Code of the Tokyo Round. The panel could not determine if the EC subsidies violated the agreement to the point that they allowed the EC to have more than an equitable share of the world market (the standard under the code). In the end, the United States granted retaliatory subsidies to U.S. wheat flour exporters.
7	E.C.	Agriculture	canned fruit	3/76 to 6/80	The National Canners Association filed a petition against the EC claiming that a variable levy imposed on canned fruit, based on the sugar content, was a barrier to trade. The case was not brought to the GATT, but during the Tokyo Round discussions, the EC agreed to switch to a fixed duty.
8	E.C.	Agriculture	soybeans and soy meal	3/76 to 1/79	The National Soybean Association filed a petition against newly imposed import requirements for soybeans by the EC. The EC required that importers pay a deposit, to be returned only if the importers purchased domestic nonfat dry milk. A GATT panel was formed, and the EC dropped this specific requirement shortly after. The soybean issue came up again in 1987 (see case #63).
9	Taiwan	Manu-factured	home appliances	3/76 to 12/77	The Lai Fu Trading Company filed a petition against a Taiwanese increase in import duties on televisions, air conditioners, and other home appliances. Taiwan claimed that it was a temporary duty for "luxury" items, necessary only because of their balance of payments crisis, and the duties would be removed as soon as the economy stabilized. The USTR again approached the Taiwanese for removal of this duty, which they then reduced to 1975 levels, and in some cases, even below.

10	E.C., Japan	Manu-factured	steel	10/76 to 1/78	The American Iron and Steel Institute filed a petition against an agreement made between Japan and the EC, which limited Japanese steel imports to the EC and thus created even more steel exports to the United States. Hearings were held, but the case was not pursued under 301.
11	E.C.	Agriculture	citrus	11/76 to 8/86	A number of U.S. citrus producers filed a petition against an import preference practice by the EC favoring citrus from certain Mediterranean countries. The USTR brought the case to the GATT, and a GATT panel ruled for a reduction in the EC tariffs for lemons and oranges by 1984, after much delay over panel membership. The EC blocked adoption of the panel report, and the United States retaliated by imposing a 40% ad valorem duty on European pasta. The EC counter to retaliated by raising tariffs on lemons and walnuts. In August of 1986, the case was resolved and the retaliatory duties removed.
12	Japan	Manu-factured	thrown silk	2/77 to 3/78	The George F. Fisher Company filed a petition alleging trade restrictions against thrown silk imports from the United States due to agreements between Japan and other exporting countries. Hearings and negotiations were held and the United States filed a GATT complaint, after which an agreement was reached to allow for an increase of U.S. imports.
13	Japan	Manu-factured	leather	8/77 to 12/85	The Tanners Council of America and the Footwear Industries of America filed petitions against Japan for quotas and tariffs on the importation of leather and leather goods. A GATT panel was formed, but bilateral consultations held up the ruling. By 1982, no resolution had been reached and the GATT complaint was refiled and retaliation options were discussed in the United States. The quota was ruled illegal by the GATT, but the panel allowed Japan to expand it over time. In 1985, Japan agreed to compensate other U.S. sectors with reduced tariffs. In addition, the United States increased tariffs on Japanese leather imports. Finally, in 1986, Japan expanded its quotas.

14	USSR	Services	marine insurance	11/77 to 7/79	The American Institute of Marine Underwriters filed a petition against the Soviet government's requirement that most U.S./USSR trade be underwritten by the Soviet insurance body. An agreement was negotiated between the two countries, and the case was terminated. Some disruption to the agreement occurred after the USSR invasion of Afghanistan.
15	Canada	Services	broad–casting	8/78 to 10/84	A case was filed by U.S. television licensees against Canada's discriminatory tax deduction practices (granting tax deductions to Canadian companies advertising on Canadian broadcasts, but not to Canadian companies advertising on American broadcasts). The United States, in retaliation, passed legislation that denied tax deductions to U.S. advertisers on Canadian broadcasts.
16	E.C.	Agriculture	wheat	11/78 to 8/80	Great Plains Wheat, Inc., filed a petition against the EC's subsidies for wheat exports. The Subsidies Code under the GATT, signed in 1979, was meant to remedy the situation, and the U.S and EC agreed to monitor.
17	Japan	Agriculture	cigars	3/79 to 1/81	The Cigar Association of America and the Associated Tobacco Manufacturers filed petitions against Japanese price levels for cigars and pipe tobacco, and additional import and sales to restrictive practices. A GATT panel was formed, but negotiations between Japan and the United States held off a determination. Japan agreed to lower tariffs on these products, to allow better advertising mediums to be used and more outlets for sales. However, Japan also raised the excise tax on all tobacco products. This problem was addressed again in the 1985 tobacco case (see case #50).
18	Argentina	Services	marine insurance	5/79 to 7/80	The American Marine Underwriters Association filed a petition against the Argentinean government for requiring virtually all import and export insurance to be placed with Argentinean companies. Argentina agreed to multilateral negotiations, and the 301 investigation was suspended, but not until 1994 was this regulation dropped completely.
19	Japan	Agriculture	pipe tobacco	10/79 to 1/81	See case #17.

20	Korea	Services	insurance	11/79 to 12/80	The American Home Insurance Company filed a petition against the Korean government for discrimination against foreign insurance. The USTR threatened retaliation, and Korea then agreed to allow AHA increased access. The case was concluded, but reopened in 1985 (see case #51) because much of the agreement had not been implemented, and a more solid agreement, with specific timelines, was made.
21	Switzerland	Manufactured	eyeglass frames	12/79 to 12/80	The Universal Optical Company filed a petition against the Swiss practice of marking the gold content of sample eyeglass frames, which they claimed destroyed their marketability. Instead of winning concessions from the Swiss, the United States began to do the same, a practice already accepted in many other countries.
22	E.C.	Agriculture	sugar	10/81 to 6/82	The Great Western Sugar Company filed a petition that EC subsidies for sugar exports were in violation of the Subsidies Code. A GATT panel ruled overall in favor of the EC, with some recommendations for specific changes to their policies. The EC eventually dropped the subsidy (in favor of subsidies given directly to sugar producers, leading to another GATT complaint by the United States, boosted by 10 other countries). No ruling was made in this second case, but the United States attempted to remedy the situation by imposing duties on imported sugar and providing price supports to U.S. sugar producers in an attempt to balance the EC's advantage. In 1987, a request was made to reopen the case, but Uruguay Round negotiations were already underway, with the specific intention by the United States and other countries to address the subsidy problem.
23	E.C.	Agriculture	poultry	10/81 to 12/84	Members of the U.S. poultry industry filed a petition against EC subsidies to poultry exporters. A GATT complaint was made under the Subsidies Code (a similar complaint was filed against Brazilian subsidies). An agreement was reached between the three countries, resulting in some reduction in Brazil's subsidy, but not the EC's.

24	Argentina	Manu-factured	leather	10/81 to 11/82	The Tanners Council of America filed a second petition against Argentina's failure to implement a previous agreement that was to eliminate a ban on the export of cattle hides and to phase out an export tax. No agreement was reached, and the United States reimposed a duty on bovine leather imports.
25	E.C.	Agriculture	pasta	11/81 to 9/87	The National Pasta Association filed a petition that EC subsidies for pasta exports violated the Subsidies Code. A GATT panel was formed that ruled in favor of the United States. The United States had already imposed duties on pasta (in response to EC citrus tariffs), but removed them when the citrus case was resolved in 1986. After serious threats from the U.S. Congress, the Reagan administration negotiated an agreement with the EC to reduce these subsidies greatly.
26	E.C.	Agriculture	canned fruit and raisins	12/81 to 12/85	Several canned fruit organizations filed a petition against EC subsidies for canned fruit and raisin exports. A GATT panel ruled in favor of the United States (except with regard to the raisins), but the decision was blocked by the EC. An agreement was reached in December, 1985, under threat of retaliation, and the case was concluded. In 1988, the case was reopened due to the EC's noncompliance with the agreement. See case #71.
27	various E.C. members	Manu-factured	steel	1/82 to 11/82	The Tool and Stainless Steel Industry Committee filed the next four complaints and #33 against countries in the EC for violation of the Subsidies Code. The cases were passed to the International Trade Commission, the ITC found injury, and President Reagan issued a number of tariffs and quotas in the U.S. market to protect the industry. The EC counter to retaliated against other U.S. imports.
28	various E.C. members	Manu-factured	steel	1/82 to 11/82	See case #27.
29	various E.C. members	Manu-factured	steel	1/82 to 11/82	See case #27.
30	various E.C. members	Manu-factured	steel	1/82 to 11/82	See case #27.

31	various E.C. members	Manu-factured	steel	1/82 to 11/82	See case #27.
32	Canada	Manu-factured	subway cars	6/82 to 9/82	The AFL to CIO filed a petition against Canadian subsidies (export financing) for a subway car contract in the United States as a violation of the Subsidies Code. Consultations were held under the GATT, but the 301 case was withdrawn because of a concurrent countervailing duty charge, and an agreement made with the New York Metro Transportation Authority.
33	various E.C. members	Manu-factured	steel	1/82 to 11/82	See case #27.
34	Canada	Manu-factured	front-end loaders	9/82 to 12/82	J.I. Case Co. filed a petition against the Canadian practice of rewarding companies that exported front to end wheel loaders/parts to Canada and also had production in Canada. (Three U.S. companies that benefited from this practice requested that the petition be rejected on the grounds that the practice did not violate the GATT.) Consultations started, but the case was not pursued. Under the U.S. to Canada Free Trade Agreement, some of the financial rewards administered were addressed.
35	Brazil	Manu-factured	footwear	10/82 to 12/85	The Footwear Industries of America filed petitions against Japan, Brazil, Taiwan, and Korea due to import restrictions on footwear in these countries. The Japan case was brought to the GATT and resolved there (see case #13), Brazil claimed a serious balance of payments crisis, and consultations took place with both Korea and Taiwan. Taiwan was the most agreeable to assist footwear sales. Brazil and Korea both agreed to a reduction of import restrictions in 1984.
36	Japan	Manu-factured	footwear	10/82 to 12/85	See case #35.
37	Korea	Manu-factured	footwear	10/82 to 10/85	See case #35.
38	Taiwan	Manu-factured	footwear	10/82 to 12/83	See case #35.

#	Country	Sector	Product	Dates	Description
39	Korea	Manu-factured	steel wire rope	3/83 to 12/83	The Committee on Domestic Steel Wire Rope and Specialty Cable Manufacturers filed a petition against Korean subsidies of steel wire rope exports as a violation of the Subsidies Code, along with a dumping petition. In November 1983, the petitioner withdrew the complaint and the case was closed.
40	Brazil	Agriculture	soybean oil and meal	4/83 to 4/85	A 301 case was opened against Brazil, Portugal, and Spain in response to a petition by the National Soybean Processors Association involving unfair subsidies for exports, and import restrictions. Consultations with the three countries yielded some positive results: Brazil removed most of its subsidies (for various reasons), and Spain and Portugal, involved in E.C. accession negotiations, also reduced their subsidies, but not their quotas on imports. Focus was then placed on the EC enlargement case, #54.
41	Portugal	Agriculture	soybean oil and meal	4/83 to 4/85	See case #40.
42	Spain	Agriculture	soybean oil and meal	4/83 to 4/85	See case #40.
43	Taiwan	Agriculture	rice	9/83 to 3/84	The Rice Millers Association filed a petition against Taiwan's subsidies for rice exports. An agreement was reached between the two countries that reduced the amount of rice exported from Taiwan into world markets. In 1989 to 90, the RMA requested that a Super 301 case be opened against Taiwanese rice, without success.
44	Argentina	Services	air couriers	9/83 to 5/89	The Air Courier Conference of America filed a petition against an Argentinean restriction that mandated all international delivery of time sensitive documents be sent by Argentinean services, and other restrictions on U.S. couriers. Negotiations, and the threat of retaliation, ended the ban on these U.S. services, but additional taxes were imposed. By 1988, the taxes were reduced, and finally in 1989, an agreement was reached between the United States and Argentina to grant national treatment to each other's air courier services.

45	Taiwan	Intellectual Property	motion picture films	12/83 to 4/84	The Motion Picture Export Association of America filed a petition against Taiwan's licensing requirements (only a certain number granted per year) for motion picture films. Taiwan agreed to phase out certain quotas, and finally all quotas, and the case was concluded.
46	E.C.	Services	satellite launch-ing	5/84 to 7/85	Transpace Carriers, Inc., filed a petition against EC subsidies that protected a French commercial satellite launch firm. The case was closed, due to the recognition the industry was highly protected in many countries due to its "newly developing industry" status in the GATT.
47	E.C.	Manu-factured	fertilizer	8/84	The Fertilizer Institute filed a petition regarding the EC import restrictions against triple superphosphate, as a violation of the Technical Barriers to Trade under the GATT. Consultations began, but no agreement or resolution was reached.
48	Japan	Manu-factured	semicon-ductors	6/85 to 6/91	After a Section 301 petition was filed by the semiconductor industry, an agreement was reached and signed in 1986 between Japan and the United States. In 1987, there was concern that Japan had failed to comply with the agreement, part of which allowed for increased U.S. (and foreign) sales of semiconductors into the Japanese market, and decreased the amount of Japanese semiconductors exported to the United States. Duties were placed on Japanese exports. The duties were removed incrementally in response to compliance by Japan with the dumping portion of the agreement. Another agreement was signed in June of 1991 and the remaining duties were removed. In the following years, the United States did secure a larger share of the Japanese semiconductor agreement, but not as large a share as anticipated.

49	Brazil	Intellectual Property	computer develop-ment	9/85 to 10/89	After petitions from the computer and electronics industry, the USTR initiated an investigation into restrictions on investment and lack of copyright protection for computer software in Brazil. Negotiations began, and eventually retaliation was threatened. The passage of legislation in Brazil to protect copyrights stopped the sanctions, and some progress has been made since. In 1993, however, Brazil was identified under Special 301 as a priority foreign country for violation of intellectual property rights.
50	Japan	Agriculture	cigarettes	9/85 to 10/86	The USTR initiated an investigation into the high tariffs on tobacco products imported to Japan and restrictions on the distribution of foreign tobacco products and investments for tobacco manufacturing. The USTR concluded consultations with Japan after an agreement was made to lower tariffs and address other trade problems in this industry.
51	Korea	Services	insurance	9/85 to 8/86	A reopening of case #20. Korea was again found not to have implemented changes in insurance practices agreed to in the previous agreement. Some additional concessions were made.
52	Korea	Intellectual Property	general	11/85 to 8/86	The USTR initiated an investigation for the violation of intellectual property protection of software and Agriculture chemicals in Korea. Bilateral consultations were able to improve the situation temporarily, but Korea has been on Special 301 Watch and Priority Watch Lists since 1989.
53	Argentina	Agriculture	soybean oil and meal	4/86 to 12/88	The National Soybean Processors Association filed a petition against Argentina's discriminatory taxation of soybean products. Under negotiations, Argentina reduced the tax on soybean products, and eliminated the other, unfair trade practices with regard to soybeans. The case was concluded, but some problems remain and Argentina was brought up as a potential Super 301 priority country in 1990.

54	E.C.	Agriculture (EC expansion)	corn, sorghum, and oilseeds	3/86 to 1/87	This case involved the United States seeking compensation for lost exports resulting from Spain and Portugal joining the EC. After some negotiation and the imposition of duties on European exports to the United States, a satisfactory compensation agreement was struck, to be renewed at the end of 1990.
55	Canada	Natural Resources	salmon and herring	5/86 to 6/90	U.S. fish processors filed a petition against Canada's prohibitions on the purchase of roe and salmon. A GATT dispute settlement panel was formed, and ruled in favor of the United States. An FTA panel also ruled in favor of the United States. After threat of retaliation, Canada agreed to changes in the level of allowable exports, with some conditions.
56	Taiwan	Manu-factured	customs valuation	8/86 to 10/86	The United States claimed that Taiwan was in violation of the GATT Customs Valuation Code, and President Reagan threatened retaliation. Taiwan agreed to remove the custom valuation system in conflict by October, which it did.
57	Taiwan	Agriculture Manu-factured	beer, wine, tobacco	10/86 to 12/86	President Reagan cited a violation by Taiwan of a previous agreement on the importation of beer, wine, and tobacco, and threatened retaliation. Two months later, Taiwan agreed to lift the import ban on beer, facilitate the sale of imported products, and provide nondiscriminatory treatment to these products. Although there were some remaining trade barriers, the case was closed.
58	Canada	Natural Resources	softwood lumber	12/86 to 1/87	This case was sparked by Canadian subsidies to its softwood lumber industry. A Memorandum of Understanding was eventually signed to resolve this issue—until 1992. See case #87.
59	India	Agriculture	almonds	1/87 to 6/88	The California Almond Growers Exchange filed a petition against India for import restrictions on almonds. (There had already been six years of bilateral negotiations before the 301 case was launched.) A GATT panel was finally formed, after much stalling by India. The panel never handed down a decision because India and the United States agreed that India would increase its quotas and reduce the tariffs over the next few years.

60	E.C.	Agriculture	meat packing	7/87 to 12/88	A petition was filed by a group of American meat producers and exporters against the EC's Third Country Meat Directive. The United States brought the case to the GATT claiming that the EC applied differing health standards to domestic and imported meat products, but a panel was never established. Consultations between the EC and the U.S. led to the conclusion of the case, only to have it reopened in 1990. See case #83.
61	Brazil	Intellectual Property	pharma-ceuticals	6/87 to 6/90	The Pharmaceutical Manufacturers of America filed a petition against Brazil for denying protection of patents for pharmaceuticals. Consultations were rejected by Brazil. Retaliation against Brazil put severe limitations on imports of certain Brazilian products, and in response, Brazil filed a complaint at the GATT. In 1990, the newly elected government of Brazil agreed to introduce legislation for patent protection to its Congress. The USTR ended the increased duties placed on Brazilian products, but violations persist.
62	E.C.	Agriculture	beef	11/87 to 1/89	President Reagan threatened to retaliate against the pending imposition by the EC of its Animal Hormone Directive, which banned the sale of beef treated with hormones. Threats of retaliation were made, and EC implementation of the ban was put off a year but eventually imposed. The United States retaliated by imposing duties on imports from the EC, and some relaxation of the hormone ban occurred, but it was not withdrawn.
63	E.C.	Agriculture	oilseeds	12/87 to 1/90	See Section 301 case study, page 27.
64	Korea	Agriculture	cigarettes	1/88 to 5/88	The U.S. Cigarette Export Association filed a petition against import restrictions imposed by Korea on cigarettes. An agreement was reached between the United States and Korea to provide foreign cigarettes the same treatment as domestic cigarettes. In this case, the agreement reached favored the United States, but the U.S. producers claim that antiforeign cigarette attitudes and preferences for domestic cigarettes have precluded major inroads into the Korean market.

65	Korea	Agriculture	beef	2/88 to 4/90	The American Meat Association petitioned against Korean quotas on beef imports. The USTR took the complaint to the GATT, and a panel ruled in favor of the United States, but the decision was blocked by Korea. The United States prepared to retaliate, but finally Korea agreed to allow adoption of the agreement and an increase in imports. Full compliance was agreed to by 1997. See case #95.
66	Japan	Agriculture	citrus	5/88 to 7/88	See Section 301 case study, page 26.
67	Korea	Agriculture	wine	4/88 to 1/89	Two wine associations filed a petition against Korean import restrictions on wine. An agreement was reached between the United States and Korea in 1989 to gradually reduce the restrictions.
68	Argentina	Intellectual Property	pharma–ceuticals	8/88 to 9/89	The Pharmaceutical Manufacturing Association filed a petition against Argentina for denying patent protection of pharmaceuticals, and for discriminatory registration practices. The petition was withdrawn after agreement by Argentina to address the issue. Legislation, seen by many as inadequate, is pending in the Argentinean Congress.
69	Japan	Services	constr–uction	11/88 to 2/90	The USTR investigated Japanese practices to exclude construction services and bidding by U.S. companies. After consultations, Japan agreed to a set of written objectives. In 1991, the USTR imposed restrictions against Japanese firms in similar services for contracts with the U.S. government.
70	E.C.	Manu-factured	fabri–cated copper	11/88 to 2/90	The Copper and Brass Fabricators Council, Inc., filed a petition against the EC's restrictions on the export of fabricated copper. The case was brought to the GATT, and a dispute settlement panel was formed but was halted when an agreement was reached to withdraw the export restrictions.
71	E.C.	Agriculture	canned fruit	5/89 to 10/89	See case #26. Reopening of consultations between the United States and the EC on canned fruit subsidies. The EC agreed to lower its subsidy rates.

72	Thailand	Agriculture	cigarettes	4/89 to 11/90	The Cigarette Export Association filed a petition against Thailand's import restrictions on foreign cigarettes. A GATT panel was formed and ruled in favor of the United States. The United States threatened to retaliate, and finally the Thai government agreed to comply with the agreement.
73	Brazil	Manu-factured	import licensing	6/89 to 5/90	See Super 301 case study, page 38.
74	Japan	Manu-factured	satellites	6/89 to 6/90	See Super 301 case study, page 37.
75	Japan	Manu-factured	super-computer	6/89 to 6/90	See Super 301 case study, page 37.
76	Japan	Manu-factured	wood products	6/89 to 6/90	See Super 301 case study, page 35.
77	India	Investment		6/89 to 6/90	See Super 301 case study, page 39.
78	India	Services	insurance	6/89 to 6/90	See Super 301 case study, page 39.
79	Norway	Manu-factured	highway toll machines	7/89 to 4/90	AMTECH filed a petition against Norway's discriminatory purchasing of highway toll equipment. An agreement was reached between the United States and Norway, but further loss of contracts by AMTECH led to consultations under the GATT. The dispute settlement panel ruled against Norway, and the recommendations were adopted by the GATT. Some violations of the agreement have since been identified.
80	Canada	Manu-factured	beer	5/90 to 8/93	See Section 301 case study, page 23.
81	E.C.	Agriculture	corn, sorghum, oilseeds	11/90 to 12/90	A reopening of case #54. The USTR threatened to suspend concessions for the European Union if the previously negotiated agreement of 1/87 was not extended. One month later, after threat of retaliation, the EU agreed to extend the agreement an additional year, and both parties agreed to review the agreement in 1991. (The agreement provisions were later extended through 1994, and were included in the Uruguay Round Agreement.)

82	Thailand	Intellectual Property	books, records, and movies	11/90 to 12/91	A petition was filed by the International Intellectual Property Alliance, the Motion Picture Association of America, and the Recording Industry Association of America leading to the announcement of Thailand as a priority foreign country under Special 301. Some enforcement was made, and the USTR is monitoring. Thailand was later named a priority foreign country under Special 301 in 1991,92,93. See case #84.
83	E.C.	Agriculture	meat packing	11/90 to 10/93	A number of meat exporters filed a petition against the EC, first in 1987 (see case #60), and again in 1990 regarding EC import restrictions on American meat. An agreement was reached and additional U.S. meat to packing plants were approved by the EC for exporting.
84	Thailand	Intellectual Property	pharma– ceuticals	1/91 to 1/94	The Pharmaceutical Manufacturers Association filed a petition regarding Thailand's lack of protection for pharmaceutical patents, and Thailand was named a priority foreign country under Special 301. (In 1989, the United States had announced a withdrawal of a benefit from the Generalized System of Preferences for Thailand due to lack of copyright enforcement, and further withdrawals were threatened.) The Thai legislature passed a law that would provide added protection for intellectual property, but increased other pharmaceutical restrictions. Due to political instability/change of leadership, retaliation was put off, and eventually Thailand complied enough to be moved, in 1994, to the watch list.
85	India	Intellectual Property	general	5/91 to 2/92	The USTR identified India as a priority foreign country under Special 301. Consultations were held with India and also brought up during the Uruguay Round negotiations, both unsuccessfully. In 1992, President Clinton, suspended some of India's privileges under the Generalized System of Preferences.
86	China	Intellectual Property	general	5/91 to 1/92	The USTR identified China as a priority foreign country under Special 301. Consultations were held with the Chinese, and after threats of retaliation and counter to retaliation, an agreement was reached.

87	Canada	Natural Resources	softwood lumber	10/91 to present	The USTR opened a 301 investigation in export practices of Canadian lumber, and determined that these practices were unreasonable. In 1991, countervailing duties were imposed upon softwood lumber imports from certain provinces. Canada appealed the sanctions to the GATT. The GATT panel ruled partly in favor of the United States, but found the U.S. requirement to post bonds inconsistent with the Subsidies Code. A binational panel under the CFTA ruled against the U.S. imposed duties, and after unsuccessful appeal, they were dropped. Negotiations continue for a more satisfactory agreement.
88	China	General	market access	10/91 to 10/92	See Section 301 case study, page 21.
89	Taiwan	Intellectual Property	copyrights	4/92 to 6/92	The USTR identified Taiwan as a priority foreign country under Special 301. An agreement was reached between the United States and Taiwan to monitor protection of intellectual property rights.
90	Indonesia	Manufactured	pencil slats	8/92 to 12/92	P&M Cedar Products and Hudson ICS filed a petition claiming that Indonesian exports of pencil slats were taxed and priced unfairly to encourage domestic production. After the initial investigation, the case was not pursued.
91	Brazil	Intellectual Property	general	5/93 to 2/94	This case was self to initiated by the USTR, under Special 301, due to the lack of intellectual property protections in Brazil. Bilateral discussions (5 rounds) were held, and as part of the Uruguay Round Agreement, Brazil agreed to introduce legislation to protect intellectual property. Brazil subsequently was listed in the Special 301, Special Mention category, in 1994.

92	China	Intellectual Property	general	6/94 to 2/95	This case was self to initiated by the USTR after identification under Special 301 in 1994, with some delay to the actual investigation due to the China MFN renewal debate. After negotiations failed to reach an agreement, threats of retaliation and counter to retaliation were made. At the end of February 1995, an agreement was made between the countries, and the United States continues to monitor its enforcement. However, Chinese compliance with this agreement has remained poor.
93	Japan	Manu-factured	after market auto parts	10/94 to 6/95	As discussed in the Super 301 section, this case was initiated in correspondence with the Super 301 deadline—though not under Super 301. Negotiations included talks on Japan's restrictive auto market and its auto parts market. USTR satisfactorily resolved the issues under investigation on June 28, 1995, terminated the investigation, and decided to monitor compliance with the agreement in accordance with section 306 of the Trade Act.
94	European Union	Agriculture	bananas	10/94 to 9/95	A petition was filed by Chiquita Brands International, Inc., against import restrictions on bananas from American companies in Latin America and also against a Framework Agreement made between the EU, Colombia, Costa Rica, Nicaragua, and Venezuela (effective 1/1/95). On September 27, 1995, USTR terminated this investigation and initiated a second investigation. Two countries, Colombia and Costa Rica, have since been the subjects of 301 cases.
95	Korea	Agriculture	meat	11/94 to 1/96	A group of red meat producers filed a petition alleging nontariff barriers against U.S. meat exports to Korea. The USTR terminated investigation on July 20, 1995, following an agreement between the U.S. and Korea and will monitor Korea's implementation of that agreement. On January 22, 1996, the United States and Korea successfully concluded technical talks to ensure the implementation of the Shelf-life Agreement. Korea quickly reached an agreement after the United States threatened to challenge Korea before the WTO.

96	Colombia	Agriculture	bananas	1/95 to present	An investigation was opened after petitions were filed by Chiquita Brands International, Inc., and the Hawaiian Banana Industry Association. The petition stated that Colombian (and Costa Rican, and other countries') policies restricted the exportation of bananas to the European Union, due to the implementation of a Framework Agreement between the EU and other Latin American countries including Colombia and Costa Rica. The USTR has consultated with the governments. In January 1996, Columbia and Costa Rica signed memoranda of understanding committing to cooperate in addressing trade distortions created by the EU regime. However, in January 1996 USTR determined that despite progress, Columbia and Costa Rica's trade practices were unreasonable under the terms of Section 301. USTR is monitoring the remaining restrictions on U.S. commerce and is working to address them.
97	Costa Rica	Agriculture	bananas	1/95 to present	See case #96.
98	Canada	Services	cultural industry	2/95 to present	Country Music Television filed a petition at the end of 1994 in response to being taken off the air in Canada on January 1, 1995. Under the CFTA, cultural industries were exempted from the investment and national treatment agreements between the two countries. Many complaints have since been filed by U.S. companies hurt by Canadian cultural industries restrictions. In June 1995, CMT and the Canadian Network reached a tentative agreement-in-principle to form a new network. On February 6, 1996, the USTR determined that the Canadian broadcasting practices deny market access and are unreasonable and discriminatory. However, due to ongoing negotiations, the USTR took no retaliatory action and will closely monitor Canada's actions regarding U.S.-owned television programming authorized for distribution in Canada.

99	Japan	Manu-factured	photo-graphic film and paper	7/95 to present	Eastman Kodak company filed a petition alleging barriers to access to the Japanese market for consumer photographic film and paper. USTR asked for public comment on the issues under investigation and has requested consultations with the government of Japan. The investigation is still pending.
100	E.C.	Agriculture	bananas	10/95 to present	A new investigation on EU banana trade policy was initiated on October 5, 1995. The USTR invited public comment as well as consultation with the EU under the WTO's Understanding of Rules and Procedures Concerning the Settlement of Disputes. Honduras, Guatemala, Mexico, and Ecuador joined the United States in requesting WTO consultation with the EU. See case #94.
101	European Union	Accession	denial of benefits	10/95 to 12/95	USTR started an investigation after the European Union increased tariffs and withdrew concession on trade as a result of the accession of Austria, Finland, and Sweden into the EU. A public hearing was held on November 22, 1995. On November 28, 1995 and agreement was reached with the EU and approved by the EU council on December 22, 1995. The agreement will fully compensate the United States for increased tariffs applied in Austria, Finland, and Sweden due to their EU membership.

Source: Case summaries are drawn from semi to annual *Report(s) to Congress on Section 301 Developments Required by Section 309 (a) (3) of the Trade Act of 1974 and the 1991,92,93,94, 95, and 96 National Trade Estimate Report on Foreign Trade Barriers.* Additional information comes from Section 301 public case files in the United States Trade Representative's Office.

Appendix B

Antidumping Laws around the World

Country	First Antidumping Law Enacted	Cases Initiated by Country (1980–1993)[a]	Cases Initiated against Country (worldwide, 1981–1993)
Canada	1904	450	51
New Zealand	1905	32	18
Australia	1906	597	6
United States	1916	638	175
Japan	1920, 1991[b]	3	197
Great Britain	1921	included in EU figures	
Finland	1968	17	12
European Union	1968	411	509 (not including European countries listed on chart)
Austria	1985	7	22
Sweden	1985[b]	13	25
Mexico	1986	87	26
Korea	1986	13	117
Brazil	1988[b]	18	88
Poland	1991[b]	24	46
Colombia	1991[b]	2	7
India	1992[b]	8	31

[a] As reported to GATT Committee on Antidumping Practices.
[b] Year of first antidumping case.

Sources: Country Embassies; General Accounting Office, *International Trade: A Comparison of U.S. and Foreign Antidumping Practices* (Washington, DC: GAO, Dewey Ballantine, 1994); *Investigation No. 332-344: Economic Effects of Antidumping and Countervailing Duty Orders and Suspension Agreements*, Testimony before the USITC, November 4, 1994.

Appendix C
Overview of Legislative Issues

The legislation to implement the Uruguay Round multilateral trade agreement included the most extensive and far-reaching rewrite of U.S. antidumping legislation since 1979. As a result, even though the political makeup of both houses of Congress has changed, there seems to be considerable and understandable reluctance in Congress to wade into another major amendment to antidumping laws—most of the proposals now being raised were rejected in the drafting of the Uruguay Round legislation.

Several antidumping issues were discussed as amendments to other legislation in the 104th Congress. Three issues have received particular attention.

Short-Supply Exception

Some opponents of the antidumping laws are concerned that antidumping orders sometimes raise domestic prices for inputs and components when domestic substitutes are not yet available in sufficient quantities to meet demand. As a result of similar concerns related to the voluntary restraints on steel imports, exceptions were allowed for importing types of steel not produced in the United States. As noted in the text, similar concerns were raised by computer makers when the 1985 U.S.-Japan Semiconductor Trade Agreement was negotiated. A portion of the agreement included what amounted to a large suspension agreement on semiconductor dumping that set minimum sale prices for semiconductors in the United States and third markets. Computer makers argued that this raised their costs to the point that it was not economical to operate in the United States and put them at a disadvantage compared to their Japanese competitors. These concerns eventually quieted down, and the computer makers joined hands with semiconductor producers to support extension of an altered U.S.-Japan Semiconductor Agreement, but similar issues have arisen in potential and real dumping cases, involving products as diverse as ball bearings and flat panel computer displays.

As a result of these concerns, a number of proposals have been offered to allow dumping duties to be suspended under certain circumstances, when the dumped product is in short supply, until domestic production increased. Last year, in the drafting of the Uruguay Round implementing legislation, a heavily lobbied battle ensued over proposals for short-supply provisions. The U.S. Commerce Department opposed these proposals on the grounds they would create an impossible administrative burden on the Commerce Department in deciding if the conditions of short supply were met and conducting periodic reviews of the situation to determine if supplies were still short. Both the House Ways and Means Committee and the Senate Finance Committee, the committees of jurisdiction, rejected short-supply provisions by a large margin.

In addition to the primary concerns expressed by the Commerce Department, there are other serious concerns about a short-supply provision. The most important of these is that the analogy between the voluntary restraints on steel and the dumping cases is flawed. A policy objective of the steel import restraints, though there was discussion of countering unfair trade, was to allow the U.S. steel industry time to adjust to new market conditions. Dumping laws, in contrast, focus on combating unfair trade practices rather than allowing adjustment time. If the purpose of a program is to allow adjustment time, it makes sense to administer the program so as to avoid negative competitive impacts upon other industries; it makes little sense to make one industry more competitive while unnecessarily making another less competitive. If the purpose of a program is to combat an unfair practice, however, these exceptions make less sense. It is clearly not in anyone's interest to encourage continued dependence on unfairly priced goods or services. Further, while a voluntary restraint may flatly exclude imports from the U.S. market beyond a specified level, antidumping laws do not exclude products from the U.S. market—they merely require imported products to be sold at a nondumped price. Thus, short-supply provisions, at least as currently drafted, seem inconsistent with the underlying purposes of antidumping laws.

Economies in Transition

As mentioned in the text, the Clinton administration proposed exempting certain nonmarket economies, except for China, from U.S. antidumping laws. The rationale for this exemption was that Russia, other former Soviet republics, and Eastern European economies were planning to increase exports to the United States as a way of generating revenues and facilitating economic growth; and there was considerable concern that these economies, like China, might frequently run into antidumping complaints because of the mixed nature of the economy and heavy reliance on state-provided inputs, such as energy. The Clinton administration argued that since the development of these economies was in the United States' interest, and since direct foreign aid was unlikely to be available in sufficient quantities, access to the U.S. market could provide important support to these economies.

Under the administration proposal, U.S. antidumping laws would not apply to imports from these Economies in Transition (EITs). They would be replaced by a substitute remedy that appeared to have a higher standard for action than antidumping laws and no secure remedy—taken together, a significant weakening of U.S. antidumping laws. (The specific elements of this proposal are rumored to be under revision, but the essential thrust of the proposal is apparently unchanged.)

This proposal was also rejected by both the House Ways and Means Committee and the Senate Finance Committee, but the administration indicated that it would resubmit the proposal in the future. (The administration actually withdrew its proposal without a vote in the Senate when it became clear that it would not win a vote.)

The EIT proposal seems troubling for two reasons. First, as noted in the text, dumping by NMEs is a rapidly growing problem. Admittedly, the vast bulk of these cases involve China, but as trade with other NMEs expands, there is every reason to think similar cases will emerge. As if to prove the point, the United States and Russia were forced to negotiate a major market-sharing agreement to head off antidumping action against Russian aluminum. Other cases seem likely to follow. It seems a most unfortunate time to weaken antidumping laws that protect the U.S. market from dumping by NMEs.

Second, if the goal of U.S. policy is to move these economies to a market footing, it seems entirely counterproductive to allow them to ignore the pricing mechanism—the principal means through which economic signals are sent in a market economy. Instead of weakening the fundamental relationship in the free marketplace between costs and market prices—the pricing mechanism, the United States should be encouraging these economies to pay close attention to prices and avoid artificially low prices on export goods.

Duty As Cost

In the debate over the Uruguay Round implementing legislation, many proposals were made to strengthen U.S. antidumping laws, and a number of them were completely or partially accepted. No single provision has become a focus for future legislative efforts to this point, but if experience is any guide, there is little doubt that substantial efforts will be made again to include provisions to make antidumping laws stronger.

One amendment that would be an obvious candidate is known as "duty absorption" or "duty as a cost." This proposal, which has been discussed for years, seeks to ensure that dumping duties translate into higher prices for the dumped product in the U.S. market. Concerns have been expressed by a number of petitioners that importing companies simply absorb the antidumping duty as a cost of doing business and do not raise market prices. In effect, the company found to be dumping would respond to the antidumping order by actually *increasing* the magnitude of dumping. In these instances then, antidumping duties would impose a financial penalty on the dumper but would not change the prices in the marketplace—the underlying goal of antidumping legislation.

This proposal has been quite controversial. Respondent interests have argued that such a proposal, if adopted, could sharply raise antidumping duties. Petitioners counter by arguing that other countries' dumping laws—particularly the European Union's—parallel this practice, and it is explicitly consistent with the WTO. The U.S. Commerce Department has opposed the proposal, and it was not included in the Uruguay Round implementing legislation. Nonetheless, there can be little doubt it will again be raised in the legislative debate on antidumping laws.

Appendix D

International Agreements on Dumping

As tariffs have been progressively lowered through international trade agreements and many nontariff trade barriers have been eliminated, attention in international trade negotiations has increasingly focused on antidumping laws. Demonstrating this trend, both the NAFTA and the Uruguay Round multilateral trade agreement contain extensive provisions impacting U.S. antidumping laws.

The North American Free Trade Agreement[1]

The NAFTA antidumping provisions are taken almost directly from those included in the 1988 U.S.-Canada Free Trade Agreement. The NAFTA does not change the actual antidumping laws of any of the three NAFTA countries—the United States, Canada, and Mexico. In fact, the agreement expressly allows each country to maintain and amend its antidumping laws (Article 1902). The only requirement is that, if they are to apply to NAFTA trading partners, future amendments must expressly include NAFTA countries. Related to this requirement, NAFTA partners have some options for consultation on proposed changes, although they have no power to stop or alter them. Countries can also request a dispute settlement panel ruling on whether the proposed amendment is consistent with the NAFTA (Article 1903).

The NAFTA does make some important changes, however, in the way in which antidumping actions are enforced and reviewed. The United States and Canada were not required directly to change their administrative procedures for implementing dumping laws, but Mexico, which had a less open history of enforcement of dumping laws, agreed to adopt an open enforcement regime providing opportunities for input, due process, etc., modeled on procedures in the other two NAFTA countries (Article 1904, Paragraph 15). Mexico passed a new Foreign Trade Law in 1993 to implement these commitments.

Undoubtedly, the most important commitment contained in the NAFTA was to allow binding review of final antidumping and countervailing duty decisions. In the United States, the original decisions in these cases are made by the Commerce Department and the International Trade Commission (Chapter 1904). The reviews are carried out by panels drawn from rosters supplied by the national governments of the NAFTA partners. In essence, in the United States these panels fulfill the judicial oversight role formerly filled by the U.S. Court of International Trade. The panels have a stated, narrow mandate of deciding whether the administering agencies properly followed their own laws when making antidumping decisions.

In the U.S.-Canada FTA, there have been several controversial decisions leading to panels being split along national lines (U.S. panelists voting for the U.S. position and Canadian panelists voting for the Canadian position), plus allegations of bias and of overstepping standards for review. The U.S.-Canada FTA established an Extraordinary Challenge Committee (ECC) to act as a review body in cases of panel misconduct.[2] Unfortunately, some U.S. jurists on this body have expressed concern with the decisions of the ECC process.[3]

In part to address these concerns, the NAFTA included several innovations, including a preference for the use of former judges on panels, expanding the review authority of ECCs, increasing time available for ECCs, and establishing a safeguard mechanism for use in serious disputes over attempts to circumvent the panels. Another provision establishes special appeal jurisdiction within the U.S. court system in the event of a challenge to the procedures' constitutionality.

The Uruguay Round Agreement[4]

Antidumping laws around the world were a major topic of negotiation throughout the Uruguay Round. Many countries—especially Asian countries—put a high priority in the negotiations on limiting U.S. and European antidumping laws. In the closing days of the negotiations in 1993, the United States made it clear that the primary, remaining U.S. objective was negotiating changes in the working draft of the agreement to preserve the effectiveness of U.S. antidumping laws. The

United States made substantial progress in this regard, but the agreement still required amendments to U.S. antidumping laws in literally dozens of areas. Below are listed what the author considers the most significant provisions of the Uruguay Round text; the list is not intended to be exhaustive:[5]

Sunset. The Uruguay Round Agreement required dumping orders to sunset after five years unless the appropriate administrative authority determined that lifting the duty "would be likely to lead to continuation or recurrence of dumping and injury." This was a substantial change from the previous U.S. practice, which was to leave the dumping order in place until the party subject to the dumping order could demonstrate that the dumping and/or injury would not recur. (Article 11.3.)

Start-up Costs. One argument that has been used against antidumping laws has been that the costs of products are naturally higher at the outset when there is a smaller volume of production over which to distribute fixed costs, and at this point it is normal business practice to sell below full cost. The Uruguay Round sought to address this by requiring antidumping laws "appropriately" to make allowances for start-up costs. (Article 2.3.1.1.)

Anticircumvention. Perhaps the most significant issue ignored in the Uruguay Round text was that of anticircumvention. There has been concern for years in the United States that antidumping orders were sometimes circumvented by the respondent companies making minor changes in the dumped product or a change in the country of origin. U.S. law includes provisions to address this problem, applying antidumping duties on the product subject to the dumping order and also to "like-products"—usually interpreted quite narrowly. After a heated dispute in the negotiations, all reference to the concept of anticircumvention was dropped in the text, although it is referenced in the Ministerial Statement accompanying the Uruguay Round.

Standing. It has been argued that dumping cases have sometimes been brought by a small portion of the domestic industry involved in a dumping case, while the majority did not support the action. The Uruguay Round Agreement requires national authorities to confirm support of the majority of an industry that expresses an opinion before initiating action. In no case can action be taken unless 25 percent of an industry expressly supports the action (often many industry groups express no position on a dumping action). The Uruguay Round does allow certified trade unions to initiate antidumping cases. (Article 5.4.)

Dispute Resolution and Dispute Settlement. In implementing the antidumping provisions of the U.S.-Canada FTA, the dispute settlement procedures ultimately proved far more significant than specific provisions. In the Uruguay Round, more substantive, specific changes have been required, but the dispute settlement procedures may ultimately prove more significant than the specific provisions. In recent GATT decisions (there is not yet a sufficient record to evaluate the WTO's performance), the most significant development has been the tendency of some dispute settlement panels to adopt a *very* restrictive view of antidumping provisions, to declare antidumping duties to be a derogation from GATT principles, and to overturn administrative decisions on what can best be called minor "technicalities."

The most important change in the WTO process is that dispute settlement procedures have been strengthened in a number of ways. Most notably, a single country can no longer block the adoption of a dispute settlement panel ruling, as was the case in the GATT.

Partially due to the increased power of dispute settlement panels, the scope of review for panels in antidumping cases was explicitly limited. Panels cannot overturn the decisions of national authorities if they have properly established the facts and evaluated them in an "unbiased and objective" manner. Of course, the U.S.-Canada FTA panels were also given a very narrow mandate, but they have been accused of exceeding it. Only time will tell how closely WTO panels stick to their narrow mandate. (Article 17.5.)

Duty As Cost. As noted in Appendix C, the Uruguay Round agreement allows duties, at the behest of the European Union, to be increased beyond the dumping margin in those cases where the importing party is related to the dumper, to ensure that the market price of the dumped good increases to reflect the dumping duty. The United States did not alter its antidumping law to utilize this provision. (Article 9.3.)

Below-Cost Sales. The Uruguay Round Agreement endorses the U.S. practice of excluding sales made below cost in the home market from the home-market price used to calculate the dumping margin. The agreement sets conditions under which these sales can be disregarded, closely paralleling those established in U.S. law some years ago. (Article 2.2.1.)

Price Averaging. The agreement provides that dumping margins will "normally" be calculated by comparing a weighted average normal value with a weighted average of export sales, or comparison of normal values with export prices on a transaction-to-transaction basis, to ensure a meaningful "apples-to-apples" comparison. This provision was aimed at certain U.S. price comparisons but still allows the U.S. practice of selecting specific export prices for comparison if "the authorities find a pattern of export prices which differ significantly among different purchasers, regions or time periods, and if an explanation is provided why such differences cannot be taken into account appropriately by the use of a weighted-average-to-weighted average or a transaction-to-transaction comparison." (Article 2.4.)

De Minimis Margins, Import Volume Levels. The agreement establishes new thresholds for size of the dumping margin (2 percent) and the volume of imports (3 percent of total imports) that must be met in order for there to be an affirmative antidumping determination. (Article 5.8.)

Notes

1. North American Free Trade Agreement provisions from: U.S. Government Printing Office, *North American Free Trade Agreement Texts of Agreement, Implementing Bill Statement of Administrative Action, and Required Supporting Statements*, (Washington, DC: GPO, November 3, 1993).

2. Judith Bello and Alan F. Holmer, *Guide to the U.S.-Canada Free-Trade Agreement* (New Jersey: Prentice Hall Law and Business, 1990), 814–15.

3. "Dissenting Opinion of United States Circuit Court Judge (Ret.) Malcolm Wilkey," *Extraordinary Challenge Committee Review Under United States–Canada Free Trade Agreement*, ECC-94-1904-01USA.

4. Uruguay Round provisions from: Office of the U.S. Trade Representative, *Final Texts of the GATT Uruguay Round Agreements*, April 15, 1994.

5. Readers interested in a more exhaustive discussion of the provisions of the Uruguay Round should see: Lynn Kamarack, "Uruguay Round Agreement Makes

Substantial Changes to Antidumping Code," *East Asian Executive Reports,* March 1994, 6; Labor/Industry Coalition for International Trade, *Implementing the Uruguay Round: What Was Achieved and How To Enact It Into Law* (Washington, DC: LICIT, March 1994); and Congressional Budget Office, *How the GATT Affects U.S. Antidumping and Countervailing-Duty Policy* (Washington, DC: CBO, September 1994).

Appendix E

Legislative History of Antidumping Laws

Dumping Law	Description of:
The Antidumping Act of 1916	Similar to antitrust laws of the time, this act established penalties (private damages through court action) for the sale of goods at less than actual market value or wholesale value with the intent to destroy the U.S. industry. Intent to destroy U.S. industry proved difficult to establish.
The Antidumping Act of 1921	Passed to strengthen the 1916 act, this act initiated the use of duties based on dumping margins, and gave power to the U.S. Treasury Department to make dumping determinations, rather than going through the courts, because of concern raised by foreign companies gaining market dominance. A much looser standard of injury was set, and even the likelihood of injury was an acceptable complaint.
The Tariff Act of 1930	This act allowed for the collection of antidumping duties once the Treasury Department had established that goods were being sold in the U.S. market at less than fair value and were injurious to the U.S. industry.
The Trade Act of 1974	This changed the administrative determination of less than fair value to ensure that products are not sold below cost, rather than just less than home-market sales. It also established time limits for dumping determinations.
The Trade Agreements Act of 1979	Passed to implement the Tokyo Round Agreement (included in which was the Antidumping Code of the GATT), this act repealed the 1921 act, amended the Tariff Act of 1930 to comply with the new GATT code (procedures to apply antidumping duties), and switched the administrative jurisdiction from Treasury to Commerce.

Dumping Law	Description of:
The Trade and Tariff Act of 1984	This included changes for determining fair market price, comparing averages in the home market with the price in the U.S. market.
The Omnibus Trade and Competitiveness Act of 1988	Among other provisions, the 1988 act widened the allowable products subject to an antidumping order (i.e., parts, slightly altered products). It also allowed the USTR to request a foreign government to take action against third-country dumping if found to be injurious to the U.S. industry.
The Uruguay Round Agreements Act of 1994	Passed to implement the changes of the Uruguay Round Agreement, this act amended U.S. dumping law to comply with Article VI of the General Agreement on Tariffs and Trade, amended how fair market value is determined, enacted guidelines to evaluate start-up costs, and provided for the review of dumping duties after five years. See Appendix D for a description of the Uruguay Round Agreement provisions.

Bibliography

Arnold, James R., "The Oilseeds Dispute and the Validity of Unilateralism in a Multilateral Context," *Stanford Journal of International Law,* 1994, vol. 30:187.

Artis, M.J., and N. Lee, *The Economics of the European Union* (Oxford: Oxford University Press, 1994).

Auerbach, Stuart, "U.S. Weighs Trade Move Against Japan," *Washington Post*, March 28, 1984, 7.

———. "Trade Panel Backs U.S. on Complaint Against Japan; GATT Unit Rules That Imports of Many Agricultural Products Unfairly Restricted," *Washington Post*, November 5, 1987, E02.

———. "Japan Stalls Response to GATT Finding; Nation Tries to Block Portions of Trade Ruling," *Washington Post*, December 3, 1987, C01.

———. "The Scramble To Stay Clear of 'Super 301'; Foreign Producers Fear U.S. Trade List," *Washington Post*, April 11, 1989, E1.

———. "Hills: Threat of Unfair Trade List Effective; Countries Now More Willing to Negotiate with U.S. on Barriers," *Washington Post*, May 13, 1989, D12.

———. "U.S. Eyes Three Nations for Unfair Trading; Japan, India and Brazil May Be Cited," *Washington Post*, May 20, 1989, D11.

———. "Bush Hears Debate on Japan Trade; Advisors Dispute 'Unfair' Label," *Washington Post,* May 23, 1989, C1.

———. "Global Stakes High as Decision on Japan Trade Nears," *Washington Post*, May 25, 1989, C12.

———. "Japan Cited by Bush as Unfair Trader; Brazil, India on List: Tokyo 'Disappointed,' " *Washington Post*, May 26, 1989, A1.

———. "Hills Defends Aggressive Trade Policy; Better System Is Goal, U.S. Official Says," *Washington Post*, June 9, 1989, F2.

———. "Japan Off U.S. Unfair Trader List; India Singled Out for Possible Retaliation," *Washington Post*, April 28, 1990, D10.

———. "U.S. Won't Retaliate Against India on Trade," *Washington Post*, June 14, 1990, C1.
———. "Raising a Roar Over a Ruling; Trade Pact Imperils Environmental Laws," *Washington Post*, October 1, 1991, D01.
———. "Democrats Seek To Extend Tough Trade Law; Measure Allows Sanctions Against Nations That Don't Drop Barriers," *Washington Post*, November 5, 1991, D1.
Barfield, Claude E., "Brother of Gephardt," *Washington Post*, March 9, 1988, A25.
Barnard, Bruce, "Brittan Says His Proposal Won't Copy U.S. Trade Act," *Journal of Commerce*, December 1, 1994, 3A.
Bayard, Thomas O., and Kimberly Ann Elliot, *Reciprocity and Retaliation in U.S. Trade Policy* (Washington, DC: Institute for International Economics, 1994).
Beachy, Debra, "Local Firm Says Mexicans Dumped Steel; Executive Says Actions Have Decimated a Good Market for Texas Companies," *Houston Chronicle*, April 6, 1995, 1.
Behr, Peter, "12 Nations Are Cited on Steel Exports; Preliminary U.S. Ruling Calls Practices Unfair," *Washington Post*, December 1, 1992, B1.
———. "19 Countries Are Cited for Steel Dumping," *Washington Post*, January 28, 1993, D11.
———. "Environmentalists Find NAFTA Is No Easy Call; National Groups Remain Sharply Divided," *Washington Post*, August 24, 1993, COL.
———. "Clinton Aims a Warning Shot on Trade—Away from Japan," *Washington Post*, March 4, 1994, B1.
———. "As Trade Triumphs Fade, Clinton Faces Series of Tough Fights," *Washington Post*, May 14, 1994, C1.
———. "White House Seeks Change in Antidumping Penalties," *Washington Post*, June 25, 1994, B1.
Bello, Judith H., and Alan Holmer, "GATT Dispute Settlement Agreement: Internationalization or Elimination of Section 301," *International Lawyer*, Fall, vol. 26, 1990.
———. *Guide to the U.S.-Canada Free Trade Agreement* (New Jersey: Prentice Hall Law and Business, 1990).
Bhagwati, Jagdish, and Hugh T. Patrick, *Aggressive Unilateralism* (Ann Arbor, MI: University of Michigan Press, 1990).

Bounds, Wendy, "Fuji Photo Film Signs Accord on U.S. Pricing, Japanese Firm Will Raise Charges on Color Paper; Kodak, Konica Benefit," *Wall Street Journal*, August 22, 1994, A4.

Bradsher, Keith, "Canada Beer Dispute Flares on Eve of Trade Talks," *New York Times*, July 25, 1992, 35.

Cadbaw, R. Michael, "Intellectual Property and International Trade: Merger or Marriage of Convenience?" *Vanderbilt Journal of Transnational Law*, Spring 1989, vol. 22.

Calvani, Terry, and Gilde Breidenbach, "An Introduction to the Robinson-Patman Act and Its Enforcement by the Government," *Antitrust Law Journal*, Fall 1990, 765–75.

Chimerine, Lawrence, Alan Tonelson, Karl von Schriltz, and Gregory Stanko, *Can the Phoenix Survive? The Fall and Rise of the American Steel Industry* (Washington, DC: Economic Strategy Institute, 1994), 55–62.

Choate, Pat, *Agents of Influence: How Japan Manipulates America's Political and Economic System* (New York, NY: Simon and Schuster, 1990).

Cohn, Lynne M., "Benedict Set to Tackle Dumping of Metal by Developing Nations," *American Metals Market*, August 24, 1994, 6.

Cole, Jeff, "Boeing Contests Loan Request for Russian Jets—Plane Maker Sees Danger in Backing for Engines from Pratt and Whitney," *Wall Street Journal*, March 6, 1995, A2.

Cordray, Monique L., "GATT v. WIPO," *Journal of the Patent and Trademark Office Society*, February 1994, vol. 70.

Crutsinger, Martin, "U.S., Japan Reach Deals, Heading Off Trade War," *Commercial Appeal (Memphis)*, October 2, 1994.

D'Andrea Tyson, Laura, *Who's Bashing Whom? Trade Conflict in High-Technology Industries* (Washington, DC: Institute for International Economics, 1992).

Danforth, John C., "Trade Accord Should Be Renegotiated," *St. Louis Post-Dispatch*, February 13, 1994, 3B.

Darlin, Damon, "Japan's Farm Lobby Fighting Reforms by Exploiting National Distrust of U.S.," *Wall Street Journal*, July 7, 1988.

———, "Closing Door: South Korea Regresses on Opening Markets, Trade Partners Say," *Wall Street Journal*, June 12, 1990, A1.

Davis, Bob, "Economy: Japanese and U.S. Business Groups Propose Plan to Resolve Trade Tensions," *Wall Street Journal*, June 24, 1994, A2.

Department of Commerce, *U.S. Foreign Trade Highlights* (Washington, DC: DOC, 1990).

Dryden, Steven, *Trade Warriors* (New York, NY: Oxford University Press, 1995).

Dunne, Nancy, "U.S. Threatens WTO Complaint Against Japan," *Financial Times*, March 29, 1995, 6.

Final Texts of the GATT Uruguay Round Agreements, "Agreement on Subsidies and Countvailing Measures," Published by the GATT, October 1994.

Fors, Gunnar, "Stainless Steel in Sweden: Antidumping Attacks Responsible International Citizenship," *Antidumping: How It Works and Who Gets Hurt,* editor: J.Michael Finger, (Ann Arbor, MI: University of Michigan Press, 1993).

Gellman Research Associates, Inc., *An Economic and Financial Review of Airbus Industrie* (Jenkintown, PA: U.S. Department of Commerce, 1990).

General Accounting Office, *International Trade: The Health of the U.S. Steel Industry* (Washington, DC: GAO, 1989).

"German Exchange Rate Scheme Found to be Export Subsidy for Airbus Parts," *Inside U.S. Trade,* January 24, 1992, 1.

Hamel, Gary, and C.K. Prahalad, "Do You Really Have a Global Strategy," *Harvard Business Review*, July-August 1985, 139.

Howell, Thomas R., Jeffrey D. Neuchterlein, and Susan B. Hester, *Semiconductors in China: Defining American Interests* (Washington, DC: Semiconductor Industry Association and Dewey Ballantine, 1995).

Howell, Thomas R., William A. Noellert, Jesse G. Kreier, and Allan Wm. Wolff, *Steel and the State* (Boulder, CO: Westview Press, 1988).

Hufbauer, Gary, and Shelton Erb, *Subsidies in International Trade* (Washington, DC: Institute for International Economics, 1984), 95–97.

Jackson, John, *The World Trading System: Law and Policy of International Economic Relations* (Cambridge, MA: MIT Press, 1994).

Joelson, Mark, "In the New Europe, A Shift in the Gears of Trade," *Legal Times*, June 20, 1994, 20.

Long, William R., "Brazil's President Moving Swiftly to Stimulate, Transform Country—Latin America: Bold Steps of the Last Six Months are Stirring Excitement and Uncertainty," *Los Angeles Times*, September 29, 1990, 16.

Maggs, John, "White House Abruptly Seeks Major Dump Law Changes," *Journal of Commerce*, June 24, 1994, 1A.

Mastel, Greg, *Trading with the Middle Kingdom* (Washington, DC: ESI, September 1995).

Mastel, Greg, and Rachel Hines, *Section 301: A Catalyst for Free Trade* (Washington, DC: ESI, April 1995).

Mastel, Greg, and Andrew Szamosszegi, *U.S. Export Programs: Business Necessity or Corporate Welfare?* (Washington, DC: ESI, 1995).

Mintz, John, "Betting It All on 777; Making a New Jet on Which Its Future Rests, Boeing Remade Itself Too," *Washington Post*, March 26, 1995, H1.

Mirow, K.R,. and H. Maurer, *Webs of Power: International Cartels and the World Economy* (Boston, MA: Houghton Mifflin, 1982).

Moskow, Michael, "Steel Industry Now Poised to Compete," *American Metals Market*, June 8, 1992.

Norman, John T., "U.S. Study Ordered of Japanese Curb on Orange Imports," *Wall Street Journal*, May 26, 1988.

Norton, Erle, and Martin Du Bois, "Foiled Competition: Don't Call It a Cartel, But World Aluminum Has Forged New Order," *Wall Street Journal*, June 9, 1994, 1.

Organization for Economic Cooperation and Development, *Arrangement on Guidelines for Officially Supported Export Credits* (Washington, DC: OECD, July 6, 1982).

Paarlberg, Robert L., *Fixing Farm Trade: Policy Options for the United States* (Cambridge, MA: Ballinger Publishing, 1988).

Pendleton, Scott, "Florida Growers Say Time Is Ripe to Stem Mexican Tomato Flow," *Christian Science Monitor*, April 12, 1995, 3.

Prestowitz, Clyde, *Trading Places: How We Allowed Japan to Take the Lead* (New York, NY: Basic Books, 1988).

Ragosta, John A., Brent Bartlett, Michael R. Geroe, and John R. Magnus, *CVD Law From the General to the Specific: Some of the*

Significant Issues and Developments (Washington, DC: Georgetown University, June 8, 1994).

Regan, Bob, "Beer Can War Not Bottled Up; Washington Spews Hints of New Action," *Amerian Metals Market,* June 17, 1993, 1.

Rowen, Hobart, "Hills Optimistic About Japanese Cooperation; Paris OECD Talks to Begin Amid Uncertainty on Trade Issue," *Washington Post*, May 31, 1989, F4.

———. " 'Gephardt II's' Meat Ax Approach to Trade," *Washington Post*, September 15, 1991, H01.

Schmitt, Bill, "Metals Industry Will Help Shape New Trade Law," *American Metals Market*, January 19, 1995, 12.

Truell, Peter, "U.S. Won't Name More 'Unfair Traders,' Sparking Some Criticism from Congress," *Wall Street Journal*, April 30, 1990, A3.

U.S. International Trade Commission, *The Year in Trade, 1993, Operations of the Trade Agreements Program* (Washington, DC: ITC, 1993).

U.S. Trade Promotion Coordinating Committee, *National Export Strategy*, October 1994, 108.

Valentine, Paul W., "Panasonic To Repay $16 Million To Settle Lawsuit," *Washington Post*, January 19, 1989, F01.

Vayle, Eric, "Collision Course in Commercial Aircraft," *Harvard Business School* case study, 1991, 7.

Viner, Jacob, *Dumping: A Problem in International Trade* (Chicago, IL: University of Chicago Press, 1923).

WuDunn, Sheryl, "U.S. Companies Slip on Way to Winter Olympics," *New York Times*, March 20, 1995, A4.

Index

A

Adversarial trade, 41-42*n.10*
Aerospace industry, subsidies in, 123, 127-133, 143
AFL-CIO, 161
Agricultural subsidies, 118, 123, 143, 149, 153, 155-160, 162
Airbus Industrie, 123, 127-133
Air Courier Conference of America, 162
Aluminum industry, dumping in, 81-82, 87
American Home Insurance, 159
American Institute of Marine Underwriters, 158
American Iron and Steel Institute, 157
American Marine Underwriters Association, 158
American Meat Association, 167
American Soybean Association, 28
AMTECH, 168
Antidumping Acts, of 1916 and 1921, 186
Antidumping duties, 72-73

Antidumping laws, 5-6, 71-105, 137
  administrative bias and, 87-88, 91*n.30*
  administrative procedures in, 73-74
  antitrust laws and, 72, 104
  consumer costs of, 100-101
  vs countervailing duty laws, 109, 140
  criticism of, 71-72, 76, 77, 100, 101
  duty absorption proposal, 178-179
  economic impact of, 98-101
  foreign, 99, 101-102, 174
  future of, 103-105
  harassment filings under, 86-87, 88-89
  international agreements and, 180-184
  legislative history of, 186-187
  nonmarket economies (NMEs) and, 81-82, 97-98, 177-178
  objectives of, 71
  as open market strategy, 93-102
  short-supply provisions and, 175-176

195

steel industry and, 79, 134, 175, 176
against market-access barriers, 95-96
See also Dumping
Antitrust laws, 71, 72, 82, 86, 98-99, 104
Argentina, 116, 158, 160, 162, 164, 167
Associated Tobacco Manufacturers, 158
Australia, 47, 99, 135, 174
Austria, 129, 173, 174

B

Belgium, 113, 129
Blair House Agreement, 27, 29-30
Boeing, 128, 133
Brazil
  agricultural subsidies of, 159, 162
  antidumping laws of, 174
  dumping of, 83, 94
  import licenses of, 34, 38-39
  import restrictions of, 161
  and intellectual property protection, 46, 48, 164, 166, 170
  as Super 301 priority, 34-35, 38
  in voluntary restraint agreement, 135
Brewing industry, import restriction in, 23-25
Britain, 120, 127, 128, 129, 174
Bush, George, 11, 21, 22, 23, 33-34, 40, 47, 135

C

California Almond Growers Exchange, 165
Canada, 120, 129
  antidumping laws of, 99, 174
  attack on U.S. trade laws, 6
  beer import restrictions of, 23-25
  dumping of, 94, 95, 155
  egg quotas of, 155
  fish import restrictions of, 165
  GATT violation of, 24-25
  lumber exports of, 170
  lumber subsidies of, 114, 116, 136-138, 143, 165
  noncompliance with bilateral agreements, 61
  subway car contract subsidy of, 161
  television broadcasting restrictions of, 158, 172
  -U.S. Free Trade Agreement, 6, 23-24, 31*n.8*, 137, 149, 181, 183
  See also North American Free Trade Agreement
Canadian International Trade Tribunal (CITT), 24, 25
Caribbean Basin Initiative (CBI), 65
Cartels, 94
Case (J.J.) Co., 161
Chicken War, 55
China
  counter-retaliation of, 67
  dumping of, 80-81, 83, 94, 97
  forced technology transfer in, 64

China *(continued)*
  in intellectual property
    agreement, 46, 47-48, 169,
    171
  market access in, 21-23
  noncompliance with bilateral
    agreements, 61
  outside WTO, 61-62
  and Super 301, 34
  threat of sanctions, 54-55
Chiquita Brands International,
  171, 172
Cigar Association of America,
  158
Cigarette Export Association,
  166, 168
Citrus
  import preference on, 157
  quotas on, 26-27
Civil Aircraft Code, 129-130,
  132, 133
Clayton Act, 71
Clinton, Bill
  and antidumping laws, 97-98,
    177
  and subsidies, 121, 133, 152
  and Super 301, 14, 18-19, 33, 41
  and Uruguay Round, 6-7
Collor de Mello, Ferdinand, 39
Collusion, 63, 66, 88
Colombia, 172, 174
Commerce Department and
    antidumping laws, 73, 74,
    80, 87-88, 91*n*.30, 135, 176,
    181
  and countervailing duty laws,
    109, 110, 135, 136
Committee on Domestic Steel
  Wire Rope, 162

Common Agricultural Policy
  (CAP), 28
Computer industry, 37-38, 164
Congress
  activism in trade policy, 16-17
  antidumping laws in, 87, 98,
    175-176, 177
  Section 301 in, 17-19
  subsidies in, 129, 131, 143
  Super 301 in, 49
Constitution, trade policy and,
  16
Copper and Brass Fabricators
  Council, 167
Copyright protection, 164, 170
Costa Rica, 172
Costs
  sales below, 78, 80, 89*n*.2, 93
  variable and fixed, 77
Countervailing duty laws, 5-6,
  79-80, 109-153
  administrative bias and,
    141-142
  administrative process in,
    110-111
  vs antidumping laws, 109, 140
  case studies, 127-138
  criticism of, 125
  general availability standard,
    114-115
  history of, 110, 113
  Subsidies Agreement and,
    148-149
  support for, 109-110
  weaknesses of, 142-143
  See also Subsidies
Country Music Television, 172
Currency, dumping and, 90*n*.14
Customs Service, 73

198 Index

D

Daimler Benz, 131
Danforth, John, 57-58
Delta Steamship Lines, 155
Denmark, 129
Dillon Round, 28
Discriminatory pricing, 72, 82, 83, 84, 89*n*.2, 104
Disinvestment, 94
DRAMs, 85
Drucker, Peter, 41*n*.10
Dumping
  counter-dumping, 82-83, 94
  defined, 72
  determination of, 73-74
  vs disinvestment, 94
  government-supported, 79-82
  NAFTA and, 23-24, 88
  overcapacity, 77-79, 93, 99
  predatory, 84-86
  tactical, 82-84
  See also Antidumping laws

E

Eastman Kodak, 66, 83-84, 173
Economics in Transition (EIT), 97-98, 177
Ecuador, 46, 47
Egypt, 46
EPROMs, 85
European Community (EC), 6, 24, 26, 67, 78
  agricultural subsidies of, 155-160
  aircraft subsidies of, 130-133
  antidumping laws of, 99, 101, 174

European Community (EC) *(continued)*
  dumping of, 95
  export restrictions of, 167
  import preferences of, 157
  import requirements of, 156, 166
  import restrictions of, 155, 163, 169, 171, 173
  oilseeds subsidies of, 27-30
  satellite subsidies of, 163
  steel subsidies of, 160
  subsidy limitation of, 145
  threat of sanctions, 55
  variable duty of, 156
Export Enhancement Program, 143, 153
Export Import Bank, 143
Export targeting, 63
Extraordinary Challenge Committee (ECC), 181

F

Fair competition, 71
Fertilizer Institute, 163
Finland, 173, 174
First-mover advantage, 123
Fisher (George F.) Company, 157
Florida Citrus Industry, 26
Footwear Industries of America, 157, 161
Forest products. *See* Lumber industry
France, 29, 65, 120, 127, 129, 133
Free trade
  reciprocal concept of, 4, 5
  unconditional concept of, 3-5

Free trade *(continued)*
  universal support for, 3
Fuji Film, 66, 83-84

G

General Agreement on Tariffs
    and Trade (GATT), 5, 8*n.7*,
    19*n.11*, 39, 60, 88-89
  antidumping laws and, 183
  Civil Aircraft Code, 129-130, 132
  material injury under,
    111-112*n.3*
  nullification and impairment
    doctrine, 66, 124
  Section 301 cases and, 21,
    23-30, 53
  subsidies and, 113-114, 115,
    116, 117*n.2*, 121, 124,
    131-132, 134, 145-147
  See also World Trade
    Organization (WTO)
General availability subsidies,
    114-115
Generalized System of
    Preferences (GSP) program,
    40, 65
Gephardt, Richard, 17
Gephardt amendment, 17-18
Germany, 47, 94, 120, 127, 128,
    129, 131, 132
Goodyear tire company, 82-83
Government-supported dumping,
    79-82
Great Plains Wheat, Inc., 158
Great Western Malting
    Company, 155
Great Western Sugar Company,
    159

Greece, 46
Guatemala, 155

H

Heileman (G.) Brewing
    Company, 24, 25
Hills, Carla, 11, 12, 22, 33, 40,
    41
Home market, protected, 94

I

Import license, 34, 38-39
India, 46, 47, 94, 174
  import restrictions in, 165
  insurance and investment
    (foreign) in, 39-40
  and intellectual property
    protection, 169
  as Super 301 priority, 34-35,
    39
Indonesia, 170
Inspection standards, 65
Insurance, foreign, discrimination
    against, 39-40, 158, 159,
    164
Intel, 85
Intellectual property protection,
    17, 19*n.11*, 163, 164, 166,
    167, 169, 170
  in China, 46, 47-48, 169, 171
  on international trade agenda,
    63
  and Special 301, 13, 14, 44, 46,
    47
  in Uruguay Round, 44, 63
International Intellectual Property
    Alliance, 169

200   Index

International Trade Commission
   (ITC)
   and antidumping laws, 73-74,
      91*n*.30, 140, 181
   and countervailing duty laws,
      109, 110-111, 115, 116,
      134-135, 137, 140-142
Ireland, 129
Italy, 120, 129

J

Japan, 129, 135, 161
   adversarial trade of, 41-42*n*.10
   antidumping laws of, 174
   attack on Section 301, 6
   automobile parts import
      restrictions of, 34, 171
   citrus quotas of, 26-27
   dumping of, 78, 83-84, 85-86,
      94, 95, 140
   leather goods quotas/tariffs of,
      157
   noncompliance with bilateral
      agreements, 61
   photographic film access in, 66,
      83-84, 173
   in semiconductor agreement,
      163, 175
   silk import restrictions of, 157
   subsidies of, 120, 123, 134
   as Super 301 priority, 19*n*.3,
      33-34, 36, 37
   supercomputer and satellite
      procurement policy of,
      37-38
   tobacco products tariffs of, 158,
      164
   trade deficit of, 16, 26

Japan *(continued)*
   violations of GATT, 60
   wood product import restriction
      of, 35-37
Justice Department, 88

K

Kantor, Michael, 46, 67*n*.5
Korea
   antidumping laws of, 174
   dumping of, 78, 83, 94, 140
   import quotas of, 167
   import restrictions of, 161, 166,
      167, 171
   insurance (foreign)
      discrimination in, 159
   and intellectual property
      protection, 164
   steel subsidies of, 162
   and Super 301, 34, 35,
      40-41
   in voluntary restraint
      agreement, 135

L

Lai Fu Trading Company, 156
Large Aircraft Sector
   Understanding, 129
Licensing, compulsory, 64
Lockhead, 128
Lumber industry
   countervailing duties in,
      170
   imports to Japan, 35-36
   subsidies of, 114, 116,
      136-138, 143, 165
Luxembourg, 129

M

McDonnell-Douglas, 128, 129, 133
Malaysia, 46
Material injury, 111-112*n.3*
Mexico, 6, 46, 47, 66, 90*n.14*, 101, 135, 174
  See also North American Free Trade Agreement
Michelin tire company, 82-83
Millers National Federation, 156
Moskow, Michael, 23
Most Favored Nation (MFN), 21
Motion Picture Association of America, 169
Motion Picture Export Association of America, 163
Motorola, 85

N

NAFTA. *See* North American Free Trade Agreement
National Canners Association, 155, 156
National Pasta Association, 160
National Security Council (NSC), 17, 50
National Soybean Association, 156
National Soybean Processors Association, 162, 164
National Trade Estimate (NTE), 17, 40, 41
Netherlands, 129
New Zealand, 46, 174
Nonmarket economies (NMEs), dumping in, 72, 80-82, 97-98, 177-178
North American Free Trade Agreement (NAFTA)
  dumping and, 88, 180-181
  subsidies and, 142, 149
Norway, 129, 168
Nullification and impairment doctrine, 66, 124

O

Oilseeds subsidies, of European Community, 27-30
Omnibus Trade and Competitiveness Act of 1988, 13, 57, 187
Organization for Economic Cooperation and Development (OECD), 118, 145
Overcapacity dumping, 77-79, 93, 99

P

P&M Cedar Products, 170
Patent protection, 166, 169
  for products under development, 63-64
Pharmaceutical Manufacturers of America, 166
Pharmaceutical Manufacturers Association, 167, 169
Philippines, 46
Photographic film industry, 66, 83-84, 173
Poland, 46, 174
Portugal, 162
Predatory dumping, 84-86
Predatory pricing, 4, 5, 72, 84, 104

Price averaging, 184
Price discrimination, 72, 82, 83, 84, 89*n*.2, 104

R

Reagan, Ronald, 27, 131, 134, 135, 160, 165, 166
Reciprocal free trade, 4, 5
Recording Industry Association of America, 169
Ricardo, David, 3, 4
Rice Millers Association, 162
Robinson-Patman Act, 71, 82, 84
Romania, 129
Russia, 62, 81-82

S

Satellites, 38, 163
Saudi Arabia, 46
Second-best analysis concept, 125
Section 201, 8*n*.7, 134-135
Section 301, 7, 11-68, 34, 96
  bilateral negotiations under, 62
  Canadian beer case, 23-25
  case studies, 20-32, 155-173
  characterized, 11
  China market access case, 21-23
  congressional power and, 17
  criticism of, 5-6, 52-56
  European Community oilseeds case, 27-30
  Japanese citrus case, 26-27
  legislative history of, 17-19, 53
  new practices on agenda of, 62-65
  nullification and impairment concept, 66
  overview of, 13
  retaliation under, 24-25, 29, 30, 52, 54-56, 59, 66-67
  subsidies and, 131, 137, 143-144
  unilateral action under, 53-54
  violations of agreements and, 61
  and World Trade Organization (WTO), 57-60
  WTO procedures linked to, 11-12, 18
  See also Special 301; Super 301
Section 337, 8*n*.7
Section 406, 8*n*.7, 80
Semiconductor industry, 85, 100, 163, 175
Seymour Foods, 155
Sherman Act, 71
Singapore, compulsory licensing in, 64
Smith, Adam, 4, 6
South Africa, 46, 135
Soviet Union, 158
Spain, 127, 128, 129, 135, 162
Special 301
  deterrent effect of, 51
  initiating cases under, 50
  overview of, 13
  record of, 44-48
  watch lists, 14, 47, 48, 51, 58
Specialty Cable Manufacturers, 162
Standards and testing requirements, 36, 37, 38
State Department, 17, 50

Steel industry
  dumping in, 78-79, 80, 88-89, 175, 176
  subsidies in, 134-136, 160, 162
Strohs brewery, 25
Subsidies, 4, 79, 80, 94, 103-104
  in aerospace industry, 123, 127-133, 143
  agricultural, 118, 123, 143, 149, 153, 155-160, 162
  categories of, 115-116
  competitive advantage and, 122-124
  counter-subsidies, 124-125, 143
  defined, 113-115, 116, 120*n*.1
  economic effects of, 121-122
  foreign levels of, 120
  international agreements on, 145-149, 151-152, 153
  in lumber industry, 114, 116, 136-138, 143
  NAFTA and, 137, 142, 149
  oilseed, 27-30
  privatization and, 116-117
  Section 301 and, 131, 137, 143-144
  in steel industry, 134-136, 160, 162
  as trade barriers, 124, 153
  U.S. levels of, 118-119, 152
  See also Countervailing duty laws
Subsidies Agreement, 146-149, 151-152
Subsidies Code, 115, 121, 129, 132, 134, 146, 148
Sugar subsidies, 110, 159
Super 301, 23, 102*n.1*
  case studies, 34, 35-40

Super 301 *(continued)*
  comparison with Special 301, 14, 47
  criticism of, 49, 52
  deterrent effect of, 51
  extension of, 13-14, 18-19, 33
  initiating cases under, 49-50
  legislative history of, 18, 33
  narrow focus of, 21
  priority countries of, 34-35, 38, 39
  trade negotiation impact of, 40-41
  warning lists, 12, 14, 33-34, 40, 58
Sweden, 88-89, 129, 173, 174
Switzerland, 129, 159

T

Tactical dumping, 82-84
Taiwan
  agricultural subsidies of, 162
  custom valuation system in, 165
  dumping of, 83, 94
  import duties of, 156
  import restrictions of, 161, 165
  and intellectual property protection, 163, 170
  outside WTO, 61-62
  and Special 301, 46, 48
  and Super 301, 35, 40-41
Tanners Council of America, 157, 160
Tariff Act of 1930, 186
Tariffs
  counter-retaliation and, 65, 66-67
  economic effect of, 121-122

Most Favored Nation status, 21
offsetting, 71
preferential treatment, 40, 65
reciprocal concessions, 28
restrictive, 24-25, 35, 36, 37, 38
retaliatory, 5, 24-25, 29, 52-53, 54-55, 65, 66
steel industry and, 135
Technology transfer, forced, 64
Television broadcasting, Canadian restrictions on, 158, 172
Television manufacturing industry, dumping in, 85-86
Thailand, 46, 47, 48, 168, 169
Tire industry, dumping in, 82-83
Tokyo Round, 129
Tool and Stainless Steel Industry Committee, 160
Trade Act
  of 1974, 12, 13, 17, 186
  of 1979, 17, 186
  of 1984, 17
  of 1988, 17, 18, 31*n.18*, 47
Trade agreements
  bilateral, 60-61, 62
  Blair House, 27, 29-30
  Dillon Round, 28
  on dumping, 180-184
  with non-WTO countries, 61-62
  North American Free Trade, 88, 142, 149, 180-181
  subsidies and, 121, 125, 145-149, 153
  Super 301 impact on, 40-41, 58
  Tokyo Round, 129
  trade laws and, 6-7

Trade agreements *(continued)*
  U.S.-Canada Free Trade, 6, 23-24, 31*n.8*, 137, 149, 181, 183
  WTO dispute settlement and, 58-60
  See also Uruguay Round
Trade deficit, 16, 17-18, 26, 40, 61
Trade laws
  attacks on, 5-6
  nonmarket economies (NMEs) and, 80
  seldom used, 8*n*.7
  trade agreements and, 6-7
  See also Antidumping laws; Countervailing duty laws; Section 301; Trade Act
Trade negotiators, status of, 16
Trade policy
  Congressional authority in, 16-17
  countervailing duty laws in, 110, 122, 125
  executive branch in, 16
  institutional interests and, 49-50
Trade and Tariff Act of 1984, 135, 187
Trade war, 54-56
Transpace Carriers, Inc., 163
Treasury Department, 50, 86

U

Unconditional free trade, 3-5
Unilateralism, 53-54
United Arab Emirates, 46
Universal Optical Company, 159
Uruguay Round, 8*n*.7, 14, 18, 28, 29, 30, 37, 72, 133, 137

Uruguay Round *(continued)*
   antidumping laws and, 181-184
   attacks on trade laws, 6-7
   dispute settlement procedure in, 27
   implementing legislation, 175, 176, 178, 187
   intellectual property in, 44, 63
   scope of, 53-54
   Subsidies Agreement, 146-149, 151-152
   time limits in, 53
Uruguay Round Agreements Act of 1994, 187
U.S.-Canada Free Trade Agreement, 6, 23–24, 31*n.8*, 137, 149, 181, 183
   See also North American Free Trade Agreement
U.S. trade representative (USTR), 12, 13, 16-17, 22-23, 24, 25, 28, 34, 37, 38, 51n.2, 103, 134, 164, 167-173

V

Voluntary restraint agreements (VRAs), 135

W

Wealth of Nations, The (Smith), 4, 6
Williams, Linn, 52
Wood products industry, import barriers in, 35-37
World Bank, 98
World Intellectual Property Organization (WIPO), 63
World Trade Organization (WTO), 30, 53, 54, 102, 103, 142
   countries outside, 61-62
   dispute settlement of, 57-60, 183
   dumping code of, 73
   gaps in coverage, 62-65
   Section 301 procedures linked to, 11-12, 18
   Subsidies Agreement of, 132

About the Author

Greg Mastel has been vice president for policy planning and administration at the Economic Strategy Institute (ESI) since August of 1995. He joined ESI in October 1994 as a senior fellow. Mr. Mastel is also an adjunct professor at the University of Maryland UC Graduate School of Management and Technology. Before going to ESI he worked in the U.S. Senate for eight years in various posts, including chief international trade adviser to the chairman of the Senate Finance Committee's International Trade Subcommittee. While working in the Senate, Mr. Mastel was an official congressional adviser to U.S. trade negotiators and worked on issues including extension of fast-track negotiating authority, the Uruguay Round trade agreement, MFN status for China, Super 301, and the North American Free Trade Agreement. He is a member of a number of economic and trade advisory boards and holds an MBA and a Ph.D. in international economics.